The Dearly Beloved

A play

Philip Osment

Samuel French — London
New York - Toronto - Hollywood

© 1993 BY PHILIP OSMENT

Rights of Performance by Amateurs are controlled by Samuel French Ltd, 52 Fitzroy Street, London W1P 6JR, and they, or their authorized agents, issue licences to amateurs on payment of a fee. **It is an infringement of the Copyright to give any performance or public reading of the play before the fee has been paid and the licence issued.**

The Royalty Fee indicated below is subject to contract and subject to variation at the sole discretion of Samuel French Ltd.

Basic fee for each and every
performance by amateurs   Code M
in the British Isles

The Professional Rights in this play are controlled by MICHAEL IMISON PLAYWRIGHTS LTD, 28 Almeida Street, London N1 1TD

The publication of this play does not imply that it is necessarily available for performance by amateurs or professionals, either in the British Isles or Overseas. Amateurs and professionals considering a production are strongly advised in their own interests to apply to the appropriate agents for consent before starting rehearsals or booking a theatre or hall.

ISBN 0 573 01746 8

Please see page iv for further copyright information

LINCOLNSHIRE
COUNTY COUNCIL

822

THE DEARLY BELOVED

Commissioned, under the sponsorship of IBM, for Cambridge Theatre Company and first performed at The Connaught Theatre, Worthing, on 2 March, 1993 and on tour with the following cast:

Terry	Sam Cox
Dulcie	Marlene Sidaway
Caroline	Sally Knyvette
Barton	John Gillett
Matt	Lucien Taylor
Tufty	Annie Hayes
Margaret	Veronica Roberts
Elaine	Pamela Moiseiwitsch
Alaric	Peter Wight

Director Mike Alfreds
Designer Paul Dart

First London performance on 26 May, 1993 at the Hampstead Theatre (Artistic Director Jenny Topper).

COPYRIGHT INFORMATION

(See also page ii)

This play is fully protected under the Copyright Laws of the British Commonwealth of Nations, the United States of America and all countries of the Berne and Universal Copyright Conventions.

All rights including Stage, Motion Picture, Radio, Television, Public Reading, and Translation into Foreign Languages, are strictly reserved.

No part of this publication may lawfully be reproduced in ANY form or by any means—photocopying, typescript, recording (including video-recording), manuscript, electronic, mechanical, or otherwise—or be transmitted or stored in a retrieval system, without prior permission.

Licences for amateur performances are issued subject to the understanding that it shall be made clear in all advertising matter that the audience will witness an amateur performance; that the names of the authors of the plays shall be included on all programmes; and that the integrity of the authors' work will be preserved.

The Royalty Fee is subject to contract and subject to variation at the sole discretion of Samuel French Ltd.

In Theatres or Halls seating Four Hundred or more the fee will be subject to negotiation.

In Territories Overseas the fee quoted above may not apply. A fee will be quoted on application to our local authorized agent, or if there is no such agent, on application to Samuel French Ltd, London.

VIDEO RECORDING OF AMATEUR PRODUCTIONS

Please note that the copyright laws governing video-recording are extremely complex and that it should not be assumed that any play may be video-recorded for whatever purpose without first obtaining the permission of the appropriate agents. The fact that a play is published by Samuel French Ltd does not indicate that video rights are available or that Samuel French Ltd controls such rights.

CHARACTERS

(ages of characters at the beginning of the play)

Dulcie Barker, about seventy years old
Terry Barker, her son, in his forties
Caroline, late thirties/early forties, married to Barton
Barton, Dulcie's nephew, early forties. A veterinarian
Matt, mid/late teens, Caroline's and Barton's son
Elaine, late thirties. A primary school teacher
Margaret, early forties. Headmistress of the primary school
Tufty, in her forties. Margaret's friend. A driver for social services
Alaric Barker, early forties. Dulcie's son. A freelance television director

There is also Tufty's dog, Bruno. Rather than having an actual dog on stage, the actors should create him by their behaviour and responses.

ACT I   A Saturday in late August
ACT II   The next day
ACT III   The following Friday
ACT IV   Two and a half years later. The Saturday before Christmas

The action takes place in a small town in the West Country

Time — the present

NOTE: In the Cambridge Theatre Company production the actors sang rounds during the scene changes between Acts I and II and between Acts III and IV. This suggested the life of the choir.

The Dearly Beloved has evolved over the past two years in consultation with Mike Alfreds. There are a number of friends and colleagues who have read various drafts and given help and feedback to whom I would like to express my thanks. They are: Noel Greig, Lin Coghlan, Libby Mason, Ian Rickson and Martin McCrudden.

I would particularly like to thank my friend Nina Ward, who read the play as I wrote it, for living with these characters for so long and for all her help and encouragement.

PHILIP OSMENT

ACKNOWLEDGEMENTS

The extract from *The Highwayman* by Alfred Noyes is reproduced by kind permission of John Murray (Publishers) Ltd.

The extract from "Bless Your Beautiful Hide" by Gene De Paul and Johnny Mercer is reproduced by permission of CPP Belwin Europe, Surrey, England

© 1953 EMI Catalogue Partnership/EMI Robbins Catalog Inc. USA

The cover photograph shows Lucien Taylor as Matt and Sally Knyvette as Caroline

ACT I

Dulcie's house in a small town in the West Country. A Saturday in late August

A window leads on to a balcony overlooking the street. Amongst the usual furnishings are a table, chairs, and a telephone

A low light comes up on Terry, a man in his forties, who stands naked in the middle of the room. He has just had his bath. His hair is wet. He touches it and looks at the water on his hand

Dulcie, his mother, enters with a towel and his clothes. She starts to dress him in a very private ritual, starting with his underpants. She speaks quietly when she needs to but it is as if we are eavesdropping, and not everything she says needs to be heard. Dulcie sings "You Are My Sunshine" to herself as she works

Dulcie Lift.

Terry lifts one leg while Dulcie pulls the underpants over his foot

And the other one.

Terry lifts the other leg and Dulcie pulls the underpants over that foot and all the way up

And again.

Terry lifts one leg while Dulcie puts the trousers over his foot

And the other.

Dulcie puts Terry's trousers on for him as she did with his underpants

Sit. Arms out.

He sits. She puts on his vest

And your shirt. Come on.

She puts on his shirt and buttons it up

Tuck it in.

Terry tucks in his shirt while Dulcie attends to his shoes and socks

Now your shoes and socks. Lift your foot, then.

She puts the sock and shoe on one foot

And the other.

She puts on the other shoe and sock. She holds out his cardigan

Come on. That's right.

He holds out his arms so that she can put on his cardigan. She rubs his hair with the towel, then gets a comb and combs his hair

What do you want? Tea or pop?
Terry Yes.
Dulcie Terry.
Terry Yes.
Dulcie Tea or pop?
Terry Biscuit.
Dulcie Don't you want a drink?
Terry Yes.
Dulcie What do you want then?
Terry Pop.

Dulcie exits

Terry brushes his hair into a different style with his hand

Act I

Dulcie returns with a biscuit tin and the drink

Dulcie There you are. Don't make a mess.

She gives him a biscuit and then combs his hair again. She goes to the telephone and dials. She listens

It's that machine again. (*She listens*) Hallo Alaric, it's your mother. I hate this blooming thing. We were just wondering how you were. Thought you might pop down now you've finished your film. It's carnival night tonight. Got people coming round to watch from the balcony as usual—Barton and Caroline and a few others from the choir. You did say you might come down this weekend so I thought I'd try you before they all arrive — see what you're up to.

Terry Al.

Dulcie Don't think I've got anything else to tell you. Barton's bought Caroline a new washing machine so he's bringing round their old one for me to have. Don't know if I'll use it. Nothing else happening I don't think. Margaret will be here tonight—headmistress now. She's still not married.

Terry tries to listen to the telephone

Stop it, Terry. (*Into the telephone*) Just given him his bath and we've had our tea — nice chop. Remember the butcher's daughter, Elaine? She's a teacher at Margaret's school. Don't think you knew her. Younger than you. Married Harold Smale. He's a mechanic at the garage. Anyway she comes to choir, she'll be here tonight. Now, what was it I wanted to tell you?

Terry tries to take the phone

Terry wants to say hallo. (*To Terry*) Quick, it's the answerphone so just say hallo.

Terry holds the phone and listens

Say hallo.

Terry Al.
Dulcie Say, "Hallo, Alaric."
Terry Al.

She takes the telephone from him

Dulcie Well, I'd better not run up my bill. Don't know what sort of weather you've had up in London. It's been terrible down here. We're hoping it won't rain tonight. Oh, that's what I was going to tell you. This Elaine I told you about — who comes to choir — well, her daughter is carnival queen. She's a lovely girl. Well, that's it then. Don't think there's anything else. Give my love to Miranda when you see her. All right? Bye. We saw your film about Brazil with the forests and everything. Very good. Well, give us a ring. It's Mum. God bless. Mum. (*She hangs up*) Blooming answerphone.

Pause

Terry Al coming?
Dulcie No, he's not coming. He's a very busy man.
Terry When's he coming?
Dulcie He's busy.
Terry Soon?
Dulcie I don't know, Terry. Don't go on about it. Finish your drink.
Terry Biscuit please.
Dulcie No. You'll be sick. (*She goes and looks out of the window*) Lot of people out in the street already.
Terry Carnival.
Dulcie That's right. Carnival night tonight. There's some of the town band going past. They'll be late for the start if they don't get up to the car park pretty quick.
Terry Music.
Dulcie Yes. The band will be playing. Now is that Barton's car? Looks like it.

Terry blows an imaginary trumpet

That's right.

Stop it, Terry, finish your drink. Your friend Tufty will be here before you finish your tea.
Terry Tufty coming.
Dulcie Yes, Tufty's coming.

Terry starts to dance around the room

Come and sit down.
Terry Carnival. (*He tries to go out on to the balcony*)
Dulcie No. The carnival's not here yet, Terry. Now come back and sit down. We'll go out on the balcony later.

She leads him back to his seat

Terry Later.

The doorbell rings. Terry starts to dance around the room again

Tufty.
Dulcie It's not Tufty. It's Barton. Now come and sit down.

She exits to the front door

Terry goes to the biscuit tin and takes a biscuit. The telephone rings. It startles him. He looks at it and takes it off the hook

(*Off*) No, don't leave it in the hall, Barton. It'll be in the way. Bring it up and put it in the bathroom.

Caroline enters

Caroline Hallo, Terry.
Dulcie (*off*) It'll have to stay there until I can get it plumbed in. Careful. Mind the wallpaper, Matt.

Dulcie enters

Have to clear a space for it in the kitchen.

Caroline I don't know how you've managed without a washing machine all these years.
Dulcie I've always washed by hand.
Caroline Living with a vet you need a washing machine.

Barton enters

Don't we?
Barton What?
Caroline Need a washing machine for your smelly clothes. He comes back from his rounds stinking of pigs and sheep and cows.
Barton Are you sure you don't want it left on the landing, Aunty? It'll block up the bathroom.
Dulcie No. It's better in there.

Barton exits

Caroline I get him to dump everything in the machine.
Dulcie I used to use a tin bath on the stove.
Caroline Thank goodness for modern technology.
Dulcie I'll just put the kettle on.

Dulcie exits

Caroline takes out her compact and checks her appearance. Terry watches her. She notices him and pokes her tongue out at him

Barton and Matt enter

Caroline All right?
Barton I suppose so. He nearly dropped it on my foot.
Terry Matt, Matt, Matt.
Matt 'Lo, Terry.
Caroline It's heavy, isn't it, darling?
Barton He hasn't got a clue.

Pause

Caroline It will make things easier for her.

Act I

Barton Mmm.
Caroline Especially with all the sheets she has to wash.
Barton He hasn't been wetting the bed lately.
Caroline Not that we know of.
Barton Why did you mention it then?
Caroline He used to.
Barton You haven't wet the bed lately, have you, Terry?
Caroline Barton!
Barton God! You're so squeamish. Anyway, you brought it up.

Pause

Caroline You don't have to hang around here you know, darling.
Barton Aunty's making a cup of tea.
Caroline You meeting Jason?
Matt Yeah.
Barton Going to the carnival dance, are you?
Matt Dunno.
Barton All those farmers' daughters on the town looking for a good time, eh?
Matt Yeah.
Barton Why didn't they ask your band to play at the dance this year?
Matt Dunno.
Caroline They're not very imaginative, are they?
Barton I suppose you're too way out for them.
Caroline Better to be way out than dull, eh, Matt?

Dulcie enters

Dulcie Kettle won't be a minute. Are you hungry?
Caroline I hope they're not.
Dulcie Want a sandwich, Matt?
Matt No thanks.
Dulcie You sure now?
Matt Yes, thanks.
Dulcie Won't take me a minute.
Matt Don't want one, thanks.
Dulcie Got some nice ham.
Barton Go on, Matt.
Caroline He doesn't want one.

Pause

Dulcie Been trying to phone Alaric. He said he might come down.
Caroline That will be nice.
Terry When's Al coming?
Dulcie Be quiet, Terry.
Caroline We haven't seen him for ages, have we?
Barton No.
Caroline Is he bringing Miranda with him?
Dulcie I expect she's staying with her mother.

She exits

Barton Oh, very clever.
Caroline What?
Barton Reminding her how little she sees her only grandchild.
Caroline I thought he might bring her.
Matt I'm going out.
Barton You haven't had your tea.
Matt Don't want any.
Caroline Have a lovely time. Do you want a lift to Jason's later?
Barton I'm not driving him all the way to Jason's house tonight.

Matt exits

Caroline Be nice to see him.
Barton Who?
Caroline Alaric.
Barton I'm surprised he's got the time to come down here. Important fellow like him.
Caroline Oh, Barton.
Barton What?
Caroline I wish you wouldn't be so ...
Barton So what?
Caroline He's your cousin.
Barton God, you annoy me sometimes. Just because you think he's so wonderful.

Dulcie enters with a sandwich

Act I

Dulcie Here we are. Oh, where's Matt gone?
Caroline He had to meet Jason.
Dulcie Brought him a sandwich.
Caroline Is Elaine coming tonight?
Dulcie I think so.
Barton (*to Caroline*) You know very well she is.
Caroline She said she *might*.
Barton She told me she was definitely coming.
Caroline When did she say that?
Barton The other night, after choir practice.
Dulcie Her Gwen will make a lovely carnival queen.
Barton She could do with losing some weight.
Caroline Don't be horrible, Barton.
Barton She's fat.
Dulcie Elaine must be very proud.
Caroline I think she's a bit embarrassed.
Barton Don't talk rubbish. She told me she was delighted.
Caroline And she told me she was embarrassed.

The doorbell rings

Dulcie Answer that, will you, Barton? While I make the tea. It might be Margaret and Tufty.
Caroline I hope they haven't brought that dog with them.

Barton exits one way, Dulcie the other

Terry goes to the biscuit tin and helps himself to a biscuit, putting it into his mouth whole. Caroline watches him

Barton returns with Tufty, Margaret, and Bruno. Tufty has brought a bottle of sherry in a carrier bag

Barton The travellers return.
Tufty Come back, Bruno. You naughty boy. Sit.
Terry Dog! Dog!

Caroline steps back in alarm as Bruno jumps up at her

Margaret Lie down.
Tufty Hallo, Caroline.
Caroline Oh!
Tufty It's all right, he's just a bit boisterous.
Barton You're not very brown.
Tufty Too hot in India to sunbathe.

They all respond as Bruno apparently moves toward Caroline

Margaret Make him sit, Tufty. You know Caroline doesn't like dogs.
Caroline It's all right.
Barton You're looking healthy, though.
Caroline Did you have a good time?
Margaret Marvellous. We just picked up the slides from the chemist on the way over.

Bruno approaches Caroline again. They all react

    Tufty, keep him away from Caroline.
Tufty Here. Good boy.

Margaret (*to Caroline*) I wanted to leave him in the car but she wouldn't hear of it.	**Tufty** (*to Barton*) How was your holiday? Greece, wasn't it?
Caroline It's OK. Honestly.	**Barton** That's right. Very restful.
Margaret He'll get hairs on Mrs Barker's furniture.	**Tufty** Everyone told us we'd get ill in India. Proved them wrong.

Margaret Tufty, are his paws clean?
Tufty Yes, miss. Barton says you had a good time in Greece.
Caroline It was very restful.
Tufty (*to Terry*) And how are you, mister?
Barton Bruno must've missed you.
Margaret I don't think so.
Tufty Mrs Carter from the school looked after him.
Margaret He's terribly fickle.
Tufty They're very loyal actually, border collies.
Margaret Must be that bit of Alsatian then, mustn't it? (*To Bruno*) You'll go with anyone, won't you?
Terry Dog.
Margaret (*to Barton and Caroline*) Where's Mrs Barker?

Act I

Barton (*to Margaret*) Getting some tea.
Tufty (*to Terry*) That's Bruno.
Barton (*to Caroline*) Perhaps she needs some help, darling.
Caroline Who?
Barton Aunty.

Caroline looks at him

Tufty I'll go and see.
Caroline No, no.

Caroline exits

Barton Has the procession started yet?
Tufty They were still up at the car park when we went past.
Margaret They hadn't finished the judging.
Tufty Elaine was helping Gwen up onto the float. She waved and said she'd be along later.

Terry starts to choke on his biscuit

Tufty You all right, mister?

She hits him on the back. He coughs more

Margaret Mind your own business, Bruno. Sit.
Barton I'll get some water.

Barton exits

Margaret You should have left him in the car.
Tufty He doesn't like it in the car.
Margaret She's too soft on you. Yes, she is.
Tufty Couldn't leave you out there could we, old boy?
Margaret She's very naughty.
Tufty And she's bossy, isn't she?

Barton and Dulcie return with a glass of water

Tufty Something went down the wrong way. Here you are.

Terry takes the glass and drinks

Dulcie He's been at those biscuits again.
Tufty Better?
Terry Better.
Dulcie You're greedy. Tea?
Margaret ⎫ *(together)* ⎧ Lovely.
Tufty ⎭ ⎩ Please.
Dulcie Barton, I can't open the bathroom door properly with the washing machine there. I think you'd better leave it on the landing.
Barton I did say that.

He exits

Dulcie *(quietly and confidentially)* I don't really want a washing machine. I prefer to wash by hand.

Dulcie exits

Margaret starts looking at the slides

Tufty Have you missed me?
Terry Yes.
Tufty I'm back now.
Terry We going Day Centre?
Tufty Yes, next week. I'll be picking you up in the minibus as usual, won't I?
Margaret Some of these look like they're really good.

Tufty goes to look at the slides

  This is Jaipur. These must be Delhi.
Tufty Here's a good one of you.
Margaret Let's see.
Tufty It's the one in the rickshaw. *(She laughs)* That hat!
Margaret Tufty, give it to me.
Tufty Yes, miss.
Margaret It's awful. I look enormous. And you never get me when I'm smiling.

Act I   13

Tufty I wonder why.
Margaret These are all Agra and the Taj Mahal.

Terry puts on his coat

Tufty Where are you going, Terry?
Terry Day Centre.
Tufty Not today.
Margaret He misses the Day Centre during the holidays. Must get bored.
Tufty I haven't got the minibus today. Next week.
Margaret They've come out well. (*She starts to put the slides away*)

Caroline enters with some teacups

Caroline Did you take lots of pictures?
Tufty A few rolls.
Caroline Be interesting to see them.
Tufty Once you've seen one temple, you've seen them all.
Margaret Maybe we'll do a slide show.
Tufty So make sure you haven't got any free evenings.

Dulcie brings in the teapot and pours tea

Caroline Well, I'd love to see them.
Tufty There's one here you might like.
Margaret Tufty, don't you dare.

They wrestle over the slides

Dulcie (*worried that they're going to knock over the tea things*) Mind ...
Caroline I suppose you saw an awful lot of poverty.
Margaret Yes. Tufty, don't.
Dulcie Terrible.
Tufty It is terrible. so many beggars.
Margaret (*to Caroline*) The shocking thing was that apparently some parents maim their own children to make them more effective as beggars.
Tufty (*to Dulcie*) There's not really a shortage of food in India either. The problems are caused by rich landowners driving people into the cities.

Margaret The worst thing about all the poverty was the way you became hardened to it.
Tufty I didn't get hardened.
Margaret No. She says she was brought up to help out people less fortunate than herself.
Tufty Very generous, us Brummies.
Margaret She'd have given away all our money if I hadn't stopped her.
Tufty She was so strict with me. Here it is, Caroline. (*She holds up the slide to the light*)
Margaret Stop it. (*She grabs the slide and knocks the tea in Dulcie's hand*) Oh, I'm sorry.
Dulcie It's all right.

She exits to get a cloth

Margaret Now look what you've done.

She follows Dulcie out

Tufty laughs

Dulcie returns with the cloth and starts mopping up the tea

Tufty is trying to stop giggling

Margaret returns and glares at Tufty. Barton enters, followed by Elaine

Barton Look who's here. The Queen Mother.

Everyone greets Elaine

Caroline How does she look?
Elaine All right. I was going to walk some of the way beside the float but she said I was making her nervous.
Dulcie Well, you'll get a good view from there. Where's Harold?
Elaine He's driving the float. Didn't trust anyone else to.
Barton He's come round to the idea, then?
Elaine Yes.
Caroline He wasn't going to let her do it at first.
Dulcie Such a lovely girl.

Act I   15

General agreement

Elaine Nice holiday?
Tufty Yes, thanks.
Elaine You're not very brown.
Margaret Goodness me, we didn't go all the away to India to sunbathe.
Elaine No. I suppose not. Barton came back from Greece looking very tanned.
Tufty That's because Barton wants to look bronzed and handsome.
Barton (*mimicking her accent*) That's right, Tufty. I do.
Elaine You don't go brown either, do you, Caroline?
Caroline I thought I did quite well this time.
Barton But you weren't brown.
Caroline I was.
Barton She wasn't.
Elaine I just get burnt. I've got very sensitive skin.
Dulcie They say you have to be careful though now, don't they, with the sun's rays?
Tufty They do, Mrs Barker.
Dulcie Nice for you to have a rest though, Margaret.
Margaret Yes.
Dulcie You deserve it.
Margaret Do I?
Dulcie All those years looking after your father. Never having a break.
Tufty Did you get away, Elaine?
Elaine No.
Dulcie It's nice you've got a good friend like Tufty to go away with.
Elaine Harold was working.
Tufty That's a shame.
Margaret Well, I hope you're feeling fit. Ready for the new intake of infants.
Tufty Here we go.
Elaine Oh, yes.
Margaret There shouldn't be so many this year. I thought you and Mrs Carter could change rooms because her class will be bigger than yours.
Tufty The holiday's not over yet, headmistress.
Dulcie I've never even been in an aeroplane.
Elaine Me neither.

Dulcie And I've got cousins in Australia.
Margaret Really?
Dulcie Yes. My uncle Billy emigrated in nineteen twenty-eight. Went sheepshearing.
Elaine Don't know where I'd rather go, India or Greece.
Margaret I went to Greece in the sixties. I hear it's changed a lot since then.
Caroline Well, it's still very beautiful.
Margaret Oh, I'm sure.
Dulcie How many sheep do you think he sheared in one day?
Margaret I don't know.
Elaine I think I'd've liked to live in Ancient Greece.
Tufty Why's that?
Elaine Oh, I don't know. All those ideals. It must have been so pure.
Dulcie Course it was handclippers then, mind. Not electric.
Elaine Beauty and truth. People living up to ideals.
Dulcie Go on, guess.
Margaret Guess what?
Dulcie How many sheep my uncle Billy could shear in one day.
Margaret Five hundred.
Dulcie Five hundred, she said, Bart. You'd be hard-pressed to shear five hundred with electric clippers.
Margaret I don't know then.
Dulcie A hundred. A hundred sheep in one day.
Elaine Must be funny coming back here after being in those inspiring places.
Tufty It's certainly quieter here.
Margaret Never changes this town.
Dulcie A hundred sheep in one day.

Pause

Tufty I think I can hear the band.

Tufty goes out onto the balcony to look. Terry follows her

They all listen again

Dulcie Let's hope it doesn't rain.
Margaret It usually pours.

Act I   17

Tufty returns

Tufty Seems to be some sort of holdup.
Dulcie Alaric's been all over the world. Went to Greece years ago. Just after he left school, didn't he, Bart?
Barton He did.
Dulcie Nineteen sixty ... something.

Pause

He's supposed to be down this weekend.
Margaret That will be nice.
Dulcie You'll have to come round and see him this time. He always asks after you.
Caroline Of course you were all in the same year at grammar school, weren't you?
Tufty Not me. I went to secondary modern. Hated school work.
Dulcie Alaric, Barton and Margaret were all in the same form.
Elaine You were head boy, weren't you, Barton?
Dulcie No, Barton was deputy. Alaric was head boy.
Tufty And guess who was head girl.
Margaret Be quiet.
Caroline (*to Barton*) I thought you said you were head boy.
Dulcie (*to Margaret*) Of course he went to Greece with you, didn't he?
Margaret Yes.
Dulcie My memory.
Barton You wouldn't have had a very good time in ancient Greece, Elaine.
Elaine Mmmm?
Caroline Why not?
Barton Women didn't get a look-in, did they?
Elaine I don't understand.
Caroline Neither do I.
Tufty He means men were more interested in each other than in women.
Elaine Oh.
Barton It's true.
Caroline How do you know?
Barton It's well-known — Socrates, all that lot — queer as coots.
Margaret I can definitely hear something.

Margaret goes out on to the balcony

Elaine Most men aren't very interested in women.

They all look at her

    I mean they like other men's company more than women's.
Caroline Honestly. The things she says sometimes.
Elaine Don't you agree?
Caroline No.
Elaine But then, I think I prefer men's company to women's.
Caroline Oh, thank you very much.
Tufty I brought some sherry, Mrs Barker.
Dulcie There are glasses there, my dear.
Elaine I just mean there's more trust ... less competitiveness.
Tufty Barton, sherry?
Barton Yes, please.
Caroline So men make better friends?
Elaine In some ways.
Dulcie My husband was a wonderful friend to me.
Elaine They see the world differently, so they seem more exciting.
Dulcie He never spoke a cross word to me.
Barton What do you think Tufty?
Tufty We make too much of our differences. (*She pours the drinks*)
Elaine Most people in this town wouldn't even talk about things like this.
Caroline No.
Barton Caroline thinks we've got narrow minds and lead narrow lives. But that's because she was brought up in Bristol and then went to college in London. She yearns for the cosmopolitan life.
Dulcie No sherry for me, my dear. Gives me gastric.

Margaret enters

Margaret There's a cattle lorry in the way. The parade can't get through.
Dulcie That's Kingdom. He's not supposed to park it in the street. It's against the law. But his uncle is mayor, isn't he? So he gets away with it.
Barton Do you want some of Tufty's sherry?
Margaret When did you get that?

Act I

Tufty Down the off-licence last night.
Margaret No, thank you, Barton.
Tufty Here we are then. Barton.
Barton Ta.
Tufty Elaine.
Elaine Harold doesn't like people drinking.
Barton Live dangerously, Elaine.
Tufty You sure you won't have one, Mrs Barker?
Dulcie All right, just a little one.
Margaret Did you know the phone was off the hook, Mrs Barker?
Dulcie No, I didn't.
Margaret Shall I put it back on?
Dulcie Yes. (*She goes to the balcony. To Terry*) Did you take this phone off the hook?

No answer

>Alaric might have been trying to phone. (*To the others*) He's always doing that.

Tufty (*quietly; to Dulcie*) Shall I give Terry a sherry?

Dulcie shakes her head

>*Terry quickly appears*

Terry Yes, please.
Dulcie Just a little one.

Tufty pours some sherry into the glass for Terry

Barton What shall we drink to?
Tufty Love and friendship.
Dulcie Very nice.

They drink

Tufty Funny name, Alaric.
Dulcie The vicar we had during the war was called Alaric Harper. Lovely man. Then when my Alaric was born they put him in my arms and he looked so beautiful. I just thought, "You're a very special baby. I'm

going to call you Alaric."
Tufty He's younger than Terry, isn't he?
Dulcie Oh yes. Terry was three when Alaric was born.

Pause. They all look at Terry

Terry More.
Dulcie No.
Caroline There was something of Alaric's on TV lately.
Dulcie There was one about all the forests that they're chopping down.
Caroline No, it wasn't that.
Dulcie Did I tell you he'd moved to Blackheath, Margaret?
Margaret No.
Dulcie Beautiful house, apparently.
Caroline What was it about, Bart?
Barton Homelessness.
Elaine You said it was ... what was the word?
Barton Can't remember.
Elaine Facile. (*She giggles*)
Barton No, I didn't.
Elaine You did. I remember clearly.
Tufty So does he work for the BBC?
Dulcie No. What is it he is, Barton?
Barton Freelance. A freelance producer and director.

The doorbell rings

Dulcie Wonder who that is?

She exits to the front door

Tufty Perhaps it's him!

Elaine giggles

Barton That drink can't have gone to your head already.
Tufty Want another, Elaine?

Elaine holds out her glass. Margaret watches

Act I 21

Elaine It's a funny word, facile, isn't it?
Caroline Did you really say that?
Barton Probably. His programmes usually are.
Caroline They're not.
Barton No, well, I didn't think you'd agree.
Margaret The one on homelessness was excellent.
Barton I forgot this was the Alaric Barker appreciation society.
Margaret It made me very angry.
Barton Me too. Such hypocrisy.

Dulcie returns with Matt

Everyone greets Matt

Matt Kingdom's cattle lorry's in the way. Parade can't get through.
Tufty Have a sherry, Matt.
Matt Ta.
Elaine They say homelessness is caused by the break-up of the family.
Dulcie That's very true.
Caroline What do you want, darling?
Matt Got any money?
Caroline Of course.
Barton What for?
Matt I'm going to Jason's on the bus later.

Caroline gets her handbag

'Lo, Bruno. (*He crouches down to pet Bruno*)
Tufty He's always pleased to see Matt.
Matt 'Lo, boy.
Dulcie Matt always wanted a dog, didn't you?
Matt Wouldn'ta minded.
Caroline He had rabbits.
Barton Only because you wouldn't let him have a dog.

Matt leaves Bruno

Caroline Here. (*She gives Matt some money*) Are you sure you're going to be warm enough?

Barton Leave him alone. You're fussing around him like a mother hen.
Caroline It might rain.
Elaine That makes you cock of the roost.
Margaret Are you working, Matt?
Barton Good question.
Caroline You're not sure what you want to do, are you?
Matt No.
Barton I've got him an interview for a job at the stables.
Margaret Aren't you doing your A-levels?
Caroline He doesn't want to go to university so he's not sure there's a point.
Barton That's his favourite phrase — "What's the point", eh, Matt?
Matt Yeah.
Dulcie Alaric's Miranda goes to university this year.
Margaret How time flies.
Dulcie Archaeology.
Margaret Fascinating.
Caroline Matt and his friend Jason have formed a band.
Margaret Really?
Caroline Yes. They played down at the *Carpenters' Inn* last month. But we haven't been allowed to hear them.
Matt You wouldn't like it.
Dulcie You could give us a little song now, Matt.
Matt I don't know anything.
Dulcie Course you do. What about the solo you sang in church?
Matt That was years ago.
Barton He won't do anything if he thinks you want him to do it.
Caroline Hasn't got his guitar, have you, love?
Matt No.
Barton Can't you sing without your guitar? Pathetic.
Elaine Barton will give us a song, won't you?
Barton Me?
Elaine Yes.
Dulcie Barton's got a lovely voice.
Barton I'm not singing.
Dulcie What was the one you sang at the concert?
Elaine (*singing*) Bless her beautiful hide,
                Whoever she may be,
                For, oh my boy I'm telling you now,
                She's the girl for me.

Act I

Barton Very good, Elaine.
Dulcie He sounded just like Howard Keel.

Caroline laughs

Barton Oh pardon me, we didn't all go to music college. Why don't you give us a song then?

General expression of enthusiasm

Caroline I'm not warmed up.
Dulcie It's the breathing, isn't it?
Caroline What is?
Dulcie That's the secret. You can always tell Caroline's been trained to sing. She breathes properly.

General agreement. Pause

Matt Bye, then.
Caroline Have a nice time.

Matt exits

Margaret Doesn't he want to go and do a course somewhere?
Caroline He doesn't seem to, at the moment.
Barton Caroline's worried that he'll get stuck here.
Dulcie There's not much here for the young people.
Caroline (*to Barton and Margaret*) You both went to university.
Barton And she thinks we're such stick-in-the-muds because we came back.
Elaine *The Return of the Native* — I read that at school. (*She laughs*)

Pause

Dulcie We should get out there.

They all move towards the window

Tufty Better leave our glasses behind. Don't want people thinking all these members of the church choir are alcoholics.

Margaret No.

She goes out on to the balcony. The others follow her out, with Barton and Elaine last

Barton Now you've done it.
Elaine Done what?
Barton She'll be jealous now.
Elaine Why?
Barton What you said about men and women. Sounded like you prefer my company to hers.
Elaine You flatter yourself.
Barton You're tiddled.
Elaine Come on.
Barton What are you doing tomorrow afternoon?
Elaine Don't know.
Barton We're going up on the moors. Will you come?
Elaine Why?
Barton Things are easier when you're there.
Elaine Oh, thank you.
Barton What?
Elaine I thought you enjoyed my company, Barton.
Barton We do.
Elaine I'm not a referee. (*Pause*) I don't know what Gwen and the boys will be doing.
Barton Have to ask Harold's permission, eh?

Caroline enters

Caroline You're going to miss her. She's coming.

Barton goes on to the balcony

Caroline All right?
Elaine Yes.
Caroline What's he been saying?
Elaine Teasing me, as usual.
Caroline Do you fancy coming for a drive with us tomorrow?
Elaine Ummm ...

Act I 25

Caroline We're going up on the moors.
Elaine All right, then.
Caroline Don't if you don't want to.
Elaine No, I'd love to.

Tufty enters

Tufty Here she is. Quick.

Elaine and Tufty exit

Caroline starts to cry

Dulcie (*off*) Here they come.
Tufty (*off*) Wave, Terry.

Caroline sobs. There is the sound of a brass band

Alaric enters

Alaric Hallo.

Caroline looks up

Had to fight my way through the crowds.
Caroline Alaric.
Alaric Tried to phone. I couldn't get through.

The brass band music gets louder

Dulcie (*off*) Doesn't she look a picture?
Margaret (*off*) Oh no, it's starting to rain.

CURTAIN

ACT II

THE MOORS 1

Afternoon. By the river — a place to swim

Elaine and Caroline are sitting on a blanket. Matt is strumming idly on his guitar

Caroline The river looks freezing, doesn't it?
Elaine Mmm.
Caroline Are you going for a swim, Matt?
Matt Don't want to.
Caroline It's probably not that cold.
Matt Don't feel like it.
Caroline Please yourself.
Elaine Barton's still quite tanned.
Caroline He uses a sunlamp.

Pause

What's Harold doing today?
Elaine Taking Gwen out for a driving lesson.
Caroline Hope he doesn't lose his temper with her.
Elaine Why should he?
Caroline I thought he was a bit fussy about his car.
Elaine It'll be all right.
Caroline Did he mind you coming out on the moors with us?
Elaine Of course not.
Caroline I just needed someone to talk to.
Matt Can I have an apple?
Caroline Of course, darling.
Matt Ta.
Caroline What did you think of Alaric?
Elaine I don't think I like him.

Act II

Caroline Really? *(To Matt)* Perhaps your dad would like one. *(Calling to Barton)* Do you want an apple, darling?
Elaine He seemed a bit superior.
Caroline You'd like him if you got to know him.
Elaine Maybe.
Caroline Funny to think that he and Margaret were boyfriend and girlfriend.
Elaine She never talks about it.
Caroline No. I sometimes think she and Tufty are the only happy couple in this town.
Elaine Maybe.
Caroline Matt, love, go and give your dad an apple.
Matt Make him come and get it.

Caroline exits to take the apple to Barton

Pause

Elaine Don't you like swimming?
Matt It's all right.
Elaine Lovely day.
Matt Yeah.

Pause

Elaine So you've decided against going to college?
Matt Dunno.
Elaine Plenty of time, I suppose.

Pause

Matt I wanna make a record with the band.
Elaine Oh, is that difficult?
Matt Have to get a manager or a deal with a record company.
Elaine How do you do that?
Matt Send them stuff on tape.
Elaine So do you get someone to record you when you play at the *Carpenter's Inn*?
Matt No. You have to do it at a recording studio.
Elaine Oh, I see.

Caroline returns

Caroline (*to Matt*) You never want to do anything I ask you, do you?
Matt What?
Caroline So truculent.
Matt I haven't done anything.
Caroline Exactly. He says he's waiting for you to go in, Elaine.
Elaine Really?
Caroline Yes. He wants to duck you.

Elaine laughs

He obviously thinks you're more fun than I am. He didn't ask me to get in. Do you think he's in love with you?
Elaine Caroline!
Caroline He might be.
Elaine Don't be ridiculous.
Caroline I wouldn't mind.
Elaine I would.
Caroline Why? You like him.
Elaine As a friend.
Caroline All the better.
Elaine I'm not having this conversation.
Caroline Why not?
Elaine Because it's ridiculous.
Caroline Or is it too near the bone?
Matt Where's the frisbee?
Caroline Where do you think it is? In the car.

Matt exits

Elaine How can you say all that in front of Matt?
Caroline I'm sorry. (*Pause. She collects herself and prevents herself from crying*) I think I'm going mad sometimes. The way Barton looks at me. It's as if he despises me.
Elaine I'm sure he doesn't.
Caroline He accused me of undermining him last night. He says I'm not interested in his work. That I never have been. He should have married a local girl.

Act II

Elaine I don't know about that.
Caroline Of course you know what it was really about.
Elaine What?
Caroline Alaric turning up like that. He's got such an inferiority complex about him. It's ridiculous. So then he takes it out on me. (*She starts to cry*)
Elaine All marriages go through bad patches.

Matt returns with Bruno

Matt Come on, Bruno. Good dog.
Elaine Oh, there's Bruno. What's he doing up here?
Matt Dunno. Yeah, come on. (*He jumps around with Bruno*)
Elaine Margaret and Tufty must be around.
Matt There they are. Hallo! Over here.

Bruno is licking Caroline's face

Caroline Go away, Bruno. Matt, get him away.
Elaine You've got him over-excited, Matt.
Matt Come on, boy. (*He moves away with Bruno*)
Elaine You all right?
Caroline Yes. Thanks. I don't know what I'd do without you to talk to.

Bruno has the frisbee in his mouth and Matt is trying to get it back

  Margaret enters with a rucksack

Margaret Hallo, there.
Caroline Hallo.
Elaine Been for a walk?
Margaret Yes. From the top road right over the moor.
Elaine Long way.
Margaret Only took a couple of hours.

  Tufty enters and throws herself on the ground

Tufty Three. I need a fag.
Margaret Here, Bruno, lie down. We were hoping to see some deer.
Caroline Any luck?

Margaret No.
Tufty (*holding out a pack of cigarettes*) Fag anyone?
Caroline Not for me.
Elaine No thanks.
Tufty Matt?
Caroline He doesn't smoke.
Matt (*taking a cigarette*) Ta.
Margaret All this fresh air and she has to smoke.
Tufty I've had enough fresh air for one day.
Margaret Mrs Barker not here yet?
Caroline Is she supposed to be?
Margaret Yes.
Tufty And the celebrity.
Margaret After church this morning, Alaric said he was going to take her for a drive so we arranged to meet up here.
Elaine Don't you like him either?
Tufty Who?
Elaine Alaric.
Tufty Don't know him.
Caroline Elaine thinks he's a snob.
Margaret That's the last thing Alaric Barker is, a snob.

Pause

Caroline Sometimes you see the deer in that copse over there.
Elaine It's lovely up here at night.
Margaret Yes, it is.
Elaine Harold used to bring me up here when we were going out.
Caroline Very romantic.
Elaine The road was a ribbon of moonlight
Over the purple moor,
Margaret And the highwayman came riding,
Margaret
Elaine } (*together*) Riding, riding,
Elaine The highwayman came riding,
Margaret
Caroline } (*together*) Up to the old inn door.
Elaine

They giggle

Act II   31

Tufty (*to Margaret*) How do you know what it was like up here at night?

They laugh more

Barton enters in swimming trunks

Barton What's the joke?
Elaine He looks like a highwayman, doesn't he?
Caroline Does he?
Barton Who me?
Tufty Not dressed like that, he doesn't.
Barton (*to Matt*) Put that out.

Matt stubs out the cigarette. Pause

Caroline Is it cold in?
Barton It's always cold, you know that.
Caroline Get your dad the big towel, Matt.
Matt Where is it?
Caroline Where you left it. In the car.
Matt Ohhhh.

He exits reluctantly

Tufty Sorry Barton, didn't know smoking was against the rules.
Barton Not your fault.
Elaine Matt tells me wants to make a record.
Barton What?
Elaine With his band. He was talking about getting a manager or something.
Barton That's Caroline's doing.
Caroline What is?
Barton Encouraging that nonsense.

Pause

Margaret Well, does anyone want a swim? (*She gets her costume from her rucksack*)

Elaine I haven't got my costume.
Margaret Tufty?
Tufty Too cold for me. I'll watch.
Margaret Hold the towel then.

She starts to get changed

Caroline He enjoys his band.

Matt returns with the towels, etc.

Barton (*as Matt enters*) He's going to get a job.
Margaret You coming in, Matt?
Matt OK.
Caroline I think I'll come with you. (*She starts to strip down to her bathing costume underneath*)

Matt attempts to change into his swimming trunks while holding a towel around his waist. He takes every precaution to be modest and gets himself into a tangle

Caroline You sure you don't want to come in, Elaine?
Barton She hasn't got her costume.
Caroline Couldn't she borrow yours, Tufty?
Tufty Sorry, didn't bring one.
Caroline I'd've brought an extra one if I'd known.
Barton I think yours would be too big for her, darling.
Tufty Ooops, I nearly saw your bum then, Matt.

Matt is embarrassed. His underpants are stuck to his foot and he is trying to kick them off. The towel nearly slips off

Barton Look at him.
Caroline You want me to hold the towel, love?
Matt No.
Barton Nobody's watching you. Don't make such a fuss.
Caroline Barton thinks we're all too prudish. He was especially taken with the topless sunbathing in Greece.
Margaret I'm ready.

Act II   33

Caroline Me too.
Barton (*to Matt*) Hurry up.
Margaret See you in there.

Tufty whistles to Bruno

   Margaret and Tufty exit

Elaine I'll come and watch.
Barton What, and leave me here on my own?
Caroline Come on, Matt.

   Caroline and Matt exit

Elaine I think we're the same size, actually.
Barton Who?
Elaine Caroline and me.
Barton She's put on a lot of weight lately. (*Pause*) What's she been saying?
Elaine She's a bit run-down.
Barton Been trying to get your sympathy?
Elaine No.
Barton She resents me, you know.
Elaine I'm sure she doesn't.
Barton She blames me for the fact that she gave up the Music Academy and a singing career.
Elaine She's never said that to me.
Barton I don't know why she married me. She should have married someone like Alaric if she wanted to lead an arty life. She's forever comparing me with him.
Elaine That's not true.
Barton The way she looks at me. So superior. Full of contempt. As if I'm some sort of ignorant brute. And she's turned Matt against me. Encouraging him in this ridiculous idea of being a pop star.
Elaine It's what he wants.
Barton Guess what he wanted to be when he was small.
Elaine What?
Barton A vet. Always had pets. He used to come out on my rounds with me, you know. He loved it. Got spoilt rotten. The farmers used to slip

him fifty p and the wives would give him sweets and cakes and God knows what. And we used to drive over these moors together in the car singing. Of course, she hated it. Jealous. I feel as if she's stolen him from me, you know. Cow. (*Pause*) Thank God I've got you to listen to me ranting.

Pause

Elaine In marriage you have to take the rough with the smooth, Barton.
Barton Good old Elaine.

Pause

Elaine Do you think the deer will come out today?
Barton Too many people around.

Alaric and Terry enter. They have a folding chair and a blanket

Alaric Hallo, there.
Barton Alaric.
Alaric Thought it was you. And it's Elaine, isn't it?
Elaine That's right.
Alaric The mother of that very pretty carnival queen. (*Calling off*) Over here, Mum. Are Margaret and Co. here?
Barton They're having a swim.
Alaric Bet it's bracing in there.
Barton It's very invigorating.
Alaric I may go in later.

Dulcie enters carrying a bag

Here we are, Mother.
Dulcie Didn't know you were coming up here, Barton.

Alaric puts the chair up for her

Thank you, my love. Looks after me, my boy, doesn't he?
Alaric You want the blanket?
Dulcie Not in this heat. I'm boiling.

Act II 35

Alaric lays out the blanket

Barton That's a very smart car you've got there, Alaric.
Alaric Thank you.
Dulcie He drives too fast.
Barton Makes mine look like an old heap.
Alaric I thought the choir sounded very good this morning.
Barton Thank you.
Alaric Caroline was in fine form.
Barton Yes.
Alaric She should have carried on with her singing.
Elaine What about the sermon?
Alaric What about it?
Barton Our vicar probably seems a bit simple-minded to you sophisticated Hampstead types.
Alaric Blackheath actually, Barton.
Dulcie He just preaches the gospel. (*She takes drinks and food out of a bag during the following*)
Barton He believes that once you start questioning the Bible then people lose faith.
Alaric Dangerous stuff.
Elaine Dangerous, why?
Alaric Unquestioning faith in anything is dangerous.
Barton That's what we'd expect from a Bohemian.
Alaric Bohemian? That's a word I haven't heard in a long time.
Elaine Does it make our lives any better, though?
Alaric Pardon?
Elaine Questioning everything all the time.
Alaric That's an ontological question in itself.
Dulcie Juice, anyone?
Barton No thanks.
Elaine What does ontological mean?
Barton Oh, Elaine, don't show us up.
Elaine Do you know?
Barton Course I do.
Elaine What is it, then?
Barton It's about religion.
Alaric Let me see ... it's the branch of metaphysics relating to the study of the nature of existence.

Dulcie Want some juice, Al?
Alaric Not at the moment.
Terry Juice.

Dulcie hands some orange juice to Barton, who hands it to Terry

Barton Here you are.
Dulcie Don't drink it all.

Margaret, Matt, Tufty and Caroline enter with Bruno

Margaret Ah, there you are. That water is freezing.
Tufty Bruno! No!

Bruno stands among them and shakes his coat out

All Ugghhh!
Tufty You naughty boy. Sorry about that, folks.

Terry giggles and shakes himself like a dog

Margaret Brrr. Where's my towel?
Tufty Here.
Caroline Refreshing, though.

Margaret, Matt and Caroline dry themselves off

Alaric Lovely spot. Can you still see deer up here?
Margaret Sometimes.
Barton Did you ever come up here at night?
Alaric Ummmm? Yes.
Barton They used to call it Lovers' Layby.
Alaric So they did.
Matt Still do.

Pause. Terry drinks some orange juice

Elaine Do you think there were ever highwaymen on these moors?
Dulcie What she say?

Act II

Alaric Did there use to be highwaymen on these moors, Mother?
Dulcie Ooooh, I don't know. I expect so. Don't remember.
Tufty Stagecoaches were a bit before your time, weren't they, Mrs Barker?
Dulcie Just a bit, Tufty.
Elaine Funny to think it was all here before us and will be here after we've gone.

Terry belches

Caroline That's a morbid thought.
Dulcie He's going to drink all that, Barton.
Barton Terry! Not too much.
Alaric I was just saying how much I enjoyed your singing this morning, Caroline.
Caroline Oh, thank you.
Dulcie Beautiful voice.
Barton I don't think it's morbid. It's good to be reminded how insignificant we all are.
Margaret Let's hope it is still here after we've gone. That we don't destroy it all.
Barton More likely to destroy ourselves.
Tufty The planet would be better off if we did.
Margaret That's a terrible thing to say.
Dulcie It's in Revelation, isn't it? The end of the world.

Terry belches again

Dulcie Terry!
Tufty Steady, old chap.
Margaret I saw this really good programme on TV the other night about the end of the world. Did you see it, Alaric? What was it called?
Tufty *Apocalypse Then.*
Alaric Oh yes, a friend of mine made it.
Margaret It showed how from time immemorial people have thought the end of the world was coming.
Elaine I saw it too. It was really interesting.
Margaret It was very well made.
Alaric Well, he had a lot of money to make it. He's very good at fundraising and selling his ideas.

Tufty I thought it was fantastic.
Barton It was good.
Alaric Really? It didn't work for me.
Tufty Best thing I've seen on telly for ages.

Pause. Terry burps and then farts. Elaine and Tufty try not to giggle

Margaret We don't know how lucky we are.
Elaine Mmmm?
Margaret Having all this beauty around us.
Caroline Have you been to the opera lately, Alaric?
Alaric I heard Carreras in Barcelona when I was there.
Caroline How wonderful!
Alaric It was sheer magic.
Caroline You lucky thing.
Margaret Do you like Placido Domingo? He's my favourite.
Tufty Look at Matt — he's gone all red.
Margaret Tufty!
Tufty What?
Alaric (*to Caroline*) And I heard Montserrat Caballe at the Liceu as well.
Tufty (*covering her nose with her hand*) Pooh, Terry.
Margaret Stop it.
Tufty Sorry, miss.

She catches Matt's eye and starts giggling

Margaret Listening to beautiful singing can be like communing with nature.
Alaric It can.
Barton Opera leaves me cold.
Margaret We've become too far removed from nature. Don't you agree, Alaric? That's where all our problems stem from.

Matt is sitting with his head bowed trying to hide his laughter. Terry realizes that something is funny and starts to join in the laughter. He farts again, which makes Tufty, Matt and Elaine laugh more

Dulcie (*trying to keep some decorum*) Really!
Barton Man's alienation. That's ontological too, isn't it?

Act II   39

Alaric Yes.
Margaret Yes. We're alienated from the natural world.

Tufty is lying on the ground laughing helplessly

Margaret Oh, honestly ...
Tufty That's why when you go to the toilet ...
Barton What'd she say?
Margaret I've no idea.
Tufty When you go to the toilet ... (*she laughs*)
Barton What?
Tufty That's why when you go to the toilet, you say, "Nature calls." (*She lies back on the grass again, helpless with laughter*)
Elaine I'd never thought of that.

Barton and Dulcie also laugh

Margaret Are you making a film at the moment, Alaric?

This attempt at conversation makes the others laugh more. Suddenly Terry stands up and points

Terry Animals.
Dulcie What's he say?
Alaric Shhhhh. (*He points*)
Tufty What?
Alaric (*whispering*) Coming out of the wood. Six of them.
Tufty Oh, yes.

They all sit or stand in silence, entranced by the deer

The Lights dim to indicate the passage of time

                            THE MOORS 2

Late afternoon

Dulcie is asleep. Elaine is sitting and sketching. In the background Tufty, Matt, Margaret, Caroline and Terry are playing frisbee. (NB The game should not be intrusive; if this is a problem, it can move off stage so that it is still heard in the distance)

Eventually Alaric returns from having a swim and picks up his towel. He moves to Elaine and looks over her shoulder

Suddenly she becomes aware of him and is startled

Alaric I'm sorry.
Elaine It's just a sketch.
Alaric Let's see.
Elaine I'd rather you didn't.
Alaric Why not?
Elaine Because I'm not very good. (*Pause*) Enjoy your swim?
Alaric Very invigorating. (*Pause*) They were fantastic, weren't they?
Elaine Yes. Pity they didn't stay longer. The stag looks more like a horse with horns and twice as big as the tree. I was never very good at perspective.
Alaric In the end it's important to communicate what it made you feel.
Elaine Oh, you draw as well, do you?
Alaric It's what my artist friends tell me.

Pause

Elaine So you make films.
Alaric For my sins.
Elaine Must be a very exciting life.
Alaric Exciting? Maybe. I sometimes wish I did something really ordinary.
Elaine Like teaching?
Alaric Why not?
Elaine I don't know that I want to be ordinary.
Alaric I bet your work is much more useful, much more real than anything I do. People are so impressed when you say you work in television. They think you're special. But it's a terrible rat-race.
Elaine But you go all over the world, see all those different countries.
Alaric Most of the time you're worrying about your next proposal and whether anyone's going to fund it. Gets a bit obsessive. You're always on the look-out for ideas. I was watching those deer and I was thinking, "I wish I had a camera crew here." And then I was trying to decide what

Act II   41

music I'd use behind it to create the mood of mystery and wonder. It puts you at one remove all the time.

Pause

Elaine Why can't you hold on to moments like that?
Alaric How do you mean?
Elaine Well, it was like magic the way they just stood there. But then as soon as you think that, that it's magical, then ... oh, I don't know what I'm trying to say really. I'm just rambling.
Alaric No, you're not. You mean as soon as you become aware of yourself experiencing something you remove yourself from the experience.
Elaine That's it. That's exactly what I mean.
Alaric It's because we try to fix things for all eternity rather than living in the moment.
Elaine Yes.
Alaric It's like me with my filmmaking. I'm always ——
Elaine I must write it down. How did it go?
Alaric Oh, ummm, I've forgotten.
Elaine When you become aware that ... I can't remember it.
Alaric As soon as you become aware of yourself experiencing a moment ... um ...
Elaine (*writing*) "... of yourself experiencing a moment ..."
Alaric As soon as you become aware of yourself experiencing a moment then you remove yourself from the experience.
Elaine "... yourself from the experience." That's so wise.
Alaric Sometimes I even imagine that my whole life is a film. The camera's there over your shoulder shooting me in close up. Always at one remove.
Elaine I wish I could say things so clearly.
Alaric Don't put yourself down. You do that a lot, you know.
Elaine Do I?
Alaric Yes, you do.
Elaine Really?
Alaric Yes. I've noticed.

Pause

Elaine Still, it must be wonderful to make films.

Alaric Why?
Elaine It means you can express yourself.
Alaric Believe me Elaine, it's a very unhealthy world. Maybe I should move back here and be a teacher.

Barton approaches and taps Elaine on the head with the frisbee

Elaine Owww!
Barton I'm sorry.

Elaine rubs her head

Sorry, did I hurt you?
Elaine (*annoyed*) No.
Barton Aren't you going to come and play?
Elaine No, thank you.
Matt Come on, Dad.
Barton (*noticing Elaine's sketch*) Let's have a look. Oh, very good.
Elaine It's not.
Barton (*showing the drawing to Alaric*) What does the connoisseur think?
Alaric Who me? I'm no expert. But I like it.
Barton You see, Elaine? Blackheath has spoken.
Elaine (*ignoring Barton; to Alaric*) Can I draw you?
Alaric Me?
Elaine Yes, I'm better at portraits.
Alaric I'd be flattered.
Matt Dad!
Barton All right. Just wait.
Matt Throw us the frisbee back then.
Barton Don't talk to me like that.
Matt You just walked off with it.
Barton That's no reason for you to behave like that.
Matt Like what?
Barton Like a spoilt child.
Matt Selfish git.
Barton What did you say? (*He moves towards Matt threateningly*)
Caroline Barton, don't.
Barton Don't know why we brought him with us.

Act II 43

Matt I didn't want to come. She made me.
Barton Well, you're welcome to walk home. Go on.
Matt Piss off.
Barton Don't use language like that. (*He hits Matt over the head with the frisbee*)
Caroline Stop it, you two. Matt!
Matt What? It's not me, it's him. Bastard.

Matt walks off

Caroline Matt! Matt!
Barton He'll soon cool off.
Caroline I'll just go and see if he's all right.
Barton Leave him.
Caroline Where's he going?
Barton For a walk. Here, catch, Tufty. (*He throws the frisbee to Tufty*)
Caroline Matt!
Barton Stop fussing.

Tufty picks up the frisbee and stands looking after Matt with Caroline

We stopped playing?

Margaret approaches Dulcie. Elaine is still sketching Alaric on the other side of the stage

Margaret Look at Mrs Barker. She's still asleep.
Barton Getting a bit chilly now. (*He puts on a sweater*)
Dulcie (*opening her eyes*) I could do with that blanket, Barton.
Alaric I'll get it.
Barton The artist's model isn't supposed to move. (*He tucks the blanket around Dulcie*)
Caroline He's going up over the moor.
Dulcie (*to Alaric*) Ought to be getting home soon.

Alaric doesn't respond

Tufty Fancy a stroll?
Caroline Oh, yes.

Elaine Shall I come?
Caroline (*looking at Elaine; after a pause*) It's all right.

Caroline and Tufty exit in the same direction as Matt

Barton Don't be long.
Caroline (*as she goes*) We won't.
Barton Kids, eh?

Pause. Terry lies down in the grass

Dulcie How's Gwen today?
Elaine Tired. Her boyfriend brought her back from the dance at half past two. Harold's taking her out for a driving lesson today.
Alaric I still can't believe you've got a daughter that age.
Dulcie She's got three lovely children.
Elaine You've just got the one, have you?
Alaric Yes. Just Miranda. She lives with my ex-wife.
Dulcie She worships her dad.
Elaine Do you see a lot of her?
Alaric Not as much as I'd like to.
Dulcie There's nothing more important to you than your family as you get older. Be lonely without your children.
Barton Parenthood's a trial. You're well out of it, Margaret.
Dulcie Oh, but Margaret's a teacher. That's different. I mean, they're all your children, aren't they, at that school. I could never be a teacher. Don't know where you get the patience. You must be a saint.
Margaret You should see me with them some days.
Dulcie Anyway, Margaret's not lonely. She's got Tufty.

Pause

Alaric Can I scratch my nose?
Elaine Of course.

Pause

Margaret I'm just going to go and get changed.

She exits

Act II

Alaric Mother!
Dulcie What?
Alaric Did you have to do that?
Dulcie What have I done?
Alaric Nothing.
Dulcie She is a marvellous teacher. Don't know what that school would do without her.
Alaric We ought to be making a move.
Dulcie All right, all right.
Elaine I should get home as well. They expected me back at four.
Alaric We'll give you a lift.
Dulcie What am I supposed to have said, anyway?
Alaric Nothing.
Dulcie People shouldn't be so sensitive.
Alaric Come on, Mother.
Dulcie All right, I'm coming. Don't rush me. Looks like I've said something so I've got to be rushed off before I do any more damage. Oh, well, that's how it is when you're old. You're dispensable.
Alaric Don't be daft, Mother.
Dulcie Come on, then, let's get going. I'd hate to cause any more embarrassment.

Dulcie exits

Elaine starts to pack up her sketching things

Alaric Can I see it?
Elaine No. I want to finish it first.
Barton I'm sure Caroline won't be long, Elaine.
Alaric We've got plenty of room.

They continue gathering things together. Alaric folds up the chair and the blanket. Barton also starts picking up towels, clothes, etc.

Tufty runs on

Tufty Has he come back?
Barton Who?
Tufty Matt.

Barton No. Why?
Tufty We can't see where he's gone.
Barton Where's Caroline?
Tufty She thought he might have gone into the wood.
Alaric Maybe he's walking home.
Barton Too far. I'll go up and look.
Alaric You want any help?
Barton No, you go on. We'll find him.

Barton exits

Alaric He's very hard on Matt.
Elaine Yes. Pity they didn't have more children, really.
Alaric I don't think Caroline could. She was very ill having Matt, I remember.
Elaine Must be difficult being an only child.
Alaric Mmmm. We'd better not keep Mother waiting.

They start to leave

Tufty Bye.
Alaric Oh, goodbye, Tufty.

Elaine and Alaric exit

Tufty opens a can of beer. She drinks some and burps, then laughs to herself, remembering Terry's performance earlier

Margaret enters

Margaret They're all leaving.
Tufty I know. Matt's disappeared.
Margaret Is Elaine going home with the Barkers?
Tufty Think so. Her and Alaric seem to be hitting it off after all.

Margaret starts picking up her things

   Lovely day.
Margaret Yes.

Act II

Tufty sighs with satisfaction

    Well, are you coming?
Tufty We could get a lift back to the car with Barton.
Margaret It's not far to walk.
Tufty It's even less far to ride. It's nice just sitting here, looking.

Barton can be heard calling Matt, off

Margaret You sound so middle-aged sometimes.
Tufty I am middle-aged.
Margaret You don't have to talk like it.
Tufty Sorry, miss.
Margaret I wish you wouldn't keep saying that. Drives me mad.
Tufty What's got into you?
Margaret Nothing's got into me.
Tufty Upset you, has it?
Margaret What?
Tufty Seeing your ex-boyfriend.
Margaret Don't be ridiculous.
Tufty I suppose it's a bit of a comedown really, isn't it?
Margaret What is?
Tufty Ending up with someone who's just a driver for social services when you could have been married to a telly producer.

Pause

Margaret Can I have the car keys?
Tufty Don't blame me if you feel like a failure.

Margaret waits. Tufty gives her the keys

    I'm sorry.
Margaret I'll see you back at the car.

Margaret exits

Tufty is left on her own and expresses her frustration

Tufty (*to Bruno*) Here, boy. (*She strokes the dog and finishes her drink*)

She gets up and exits after Margaret

Barton and Caroline can be heard calling Matt. Terry, who has been lying in the grass, sits up and looks around, enjoying the feeling of being outside. He sings his own version of "You Are My Sunshine"

Terry   Sunshine ...
Sunshine ...
Yappy ...
Skies are blue.
Sunshine ...
Sunshine ...
'Appy, skies are blue.

Barton and Caroline can be heard calling further away now

The Lights fade

CURTAIN

ACT III
THE GARDEN 1

Early evening. The garden of Margaret's and Tufty's house

Tufty is adjusting a slide projector (practical) on a step ladder. Bruno is about the garden somewhere. On the garden table there is a punch bowl and glasses, slides and the cassette for the projector. The projector is switched on and is directed at an imaginary screen in the audience

Margaret enters with a book

Margaret Is this one thick enough?
Tufty We'll try it.
Margaret I still think this is a ridiculous idea.
Tufty What?
Margaret Showing slides in the garden.
Tufty Put it under this end.
Margaret It will be too bright out here.
Tufty Not when it gets dark. We'll put off the outside light. Be cooler anyway.
Margaret It's still not right. It needs to go up.
Tufty I know.
Margaret Adjust the legs.
Tufty They're broken. You know that. That's why I'm using the book.
Margaret I don't know why we're using your old projector.
Tufty What are Caroline and Elaine doing?
Margaret Elaine's brought a trifle round. They're putting whipped cream on the top.
Tufty Why's Elaine wearing those ridiculous sunglasses?
Margaret I don't know. (*She goes to the table and looks at the slides*)
Margaret You're not showing this one.
Tufty Which one?
Margaret The one of me getting out of the rickshaw in Agra.
Tufty Why not?

Margaret Because it makes me look enormous.
Tufty Alaric musn't see that one then.

Silence

(In exasperation with the projector) Aowhhh.
Margaret We should have borrowed the one from school.
Tufty This one's fine.
Margaret Except you can't adjust the legs.
Tufty It's a stronger bulb.
Margaret It wouldn't need to be so strong if we showed them indoors.
Tufty Pour me a drink.
Margaret Bit early, isn't it?

Tufty goes and gets herself a drink of the punch and then returns to fiddle with the projector

It's coming off the edge of the screen.
Tufty I know. *(She plays with the focus and sips her drink)*
Margaret Shall I bring the screen nearer?
Tufty No! Out of the way, Bruno. Go and lie down.
Margaret You can't adjust the lens properly with that projector either.
Tufty This is a really good projector. I paid a lot of money for it.
Margaret Twenty years ago.
Tufty Oh, shut up.
Margaret Shut up yourself.

Elaine enters wearing quite ostentatious sunglasses

Elaine Have you got any hundreds and thousands?
Tufty Pardon?
Elaine You know, to sprinkle on top of the trifle.
Margaret Vermicelli? You could grate some chocolate.
Tufty We haven't got any chocolate.
Margaret Yes, we have.
Tufty No, we haven't.
Margaret We have.
Tufty You scoffed it all the other night.
Margaret Oh yes.

Act III   51

Elaine It's all right.

Elaine exits

Tufty (*putting the slides in the cassette*) Do you want a drink?

Margaret doesn't answer

　Maggie?
Margaret Might as well.
Tufty That dress suits you.
Margaret Thank you.
Tufty She looks very tasty, doesn't she, Bruno? Cheers.
Margaret Cheers.

Tufty reaches out and touches Margaret's cheek

　Don't. (*She looks towards the house. Pause*) How much gin did you put in this?

Tufty doesn't reply

　It's very strong.

Elaine and Caroline enter

Elaine That's that done.
Caroline The food looks lovely.
Tufty Come and have some punch, you two.
Caroline I thought Barton was out here.
Tufty He's gone to have a look at the fish in our pond.
Caroline You've got a fish pond?
Margaret Don't get her started, Caroline. The hours we spend in garden centres buying plants and fish for that pond. She's even got a waterfall with lights.
Caroline How sweet. I must have a look later. Matt used to have fish.
Elaine Is Matt back yet?
Caroline No.
Tufty Where's he been?

Caroline He went up to Bristol this morning with Alaric.
Margaret Bristol?
Caroline Yes.
Elaine Alaric had to go for a meeting. He took Matt because he knows a record producer up there who's got a recording studio.
Caroline You're well-informed.
Tufty (*handing out the drinks*) There you are. (*She picks up her own drink*)
Margaret The salad's still got to be made.

Tufty exits

Caroline I thought you might have gone with them, Elaine.
Elaine Gone with who?
Caroline Alaric and Matt.
Elaine Had some preparation to do for school.
Caroline He asked you then, did he?
Elaine Who?
Caroline Alaric.
Elaine He mentioned they were going.
Caroline Thought he might have.
Margaret There's a book on special needs teaching you must read for next term.
Elaine Right.
Caroline Have you seen much of Alaric since last Sunday on the moors, Margaret?
Margaret I've been at the school getting things ready.
Caroline I thought you were old friends.
Margaret We haven't been in touch for years.
Caroline Sad how people drift apart, isn't it?

Tufty returns

Tufty The Barkers are here. They've brought Matt. Can you come and help, Maggie?

Margaret and Tufty exit

Caroline This punch is rather wonderful, isn't it?
Elaine Are you angry with me?

Act III

Caroline Why should I be angry with you?

Caroline exits

Elaine, left alone on stage, behaves in an agitated manner. She moves toward the house to see if she can see Alaric. She takes a mirror out of her handbag and looks at herself, adjusting her sunglasses. She puts on some lipstick and smiles at herself brightly

Barton enters

Elaine How are the fish?
Barton They look healthy enough to me. Not that I'm an expert. (*He looks towards the house*) I need to talk to you.
Elaine I should see if Margaret and Tufty need any help.
Barton It won't take a minute.

Tufty enters with Terry, Alaric and Matt

Tufty Here we are.
Alaric Hallo there.
Barton Hallo.
Tufty Help yourself to punch.

Alaric pours himself some punch

Look who's there under the bush, Terry.
Terry Dog.
Tufty That's your friend Bruno.

Terry sticks his tongue out and pants like a dog

Yes, he's hot.
Terry (*seeing Alaric's drink*) Drink.
Alaric All right, not too much. (*He gives Terry some punch*)
Elaine How was Bristol?
Matt Brilliant. Twenty-four track digital recording studio, everything computerized. We'll be able to do a really good demo tape.
Barton And when are you planning to do that?

Matt Monday and Tuesday.
Barton I arranged for you to go to that job interview at the stables on Tuesday.
Matt I forgot.
Elaine Won't they change it?
Barton We'll have to see.

Pause

Tufty Come on, Terry, let's go and have a look at the fish.
Terry Fish.
Tufty Shall we take Bruno with us?
Terry Yes.
Tufty Here, boy.

Terry edges around as if he is slightly scared of Bruno

Coming, Matt?
Matt Yeah.

Tufty, Terry and Matt exit

Alaric Sorry about that, Barton. Don't want to tread on anyone's toes.
Barton I'm sure you don't.
Alaric He seems pretty keen on his music.
Barton You think so?
Alaric Yes. Don't you?
Barton He hasn't got any real staying power. Bit lazy, our Matt. Needs to get some work experience.
Alaric Work isn't everything.
Barton Is that what you say to Miranda?
Alaric Yes. (*Pause*) How are you, Elaine?
Elaine I'm all right.
Barton Why didn't you bring her with you?
Alaric Miranda?
Barton Yes.
Alaric She's with her mother.
Barton Things must have been difficult in that quarter since the divorce.
Alaric Not at all. It's all quite amicable.

Act III

Barton Very civilized.
Alaric Actually, Barton, don't you think it would be good if Terry had some sort of work?
Barton Why? He's happy.
Alaric He's very dependent on Mother.
Barton He's company for her.
Alaric Mmmm. Did you get your work for school done, Elaine?
Elaine Some of it. I got a bit sidetracked.
Barton Has Miranda got over it do you think?
Alaric Got over what?
Barton The divorce. Losing her dad.
Alaric She didn't lose me. Sidetracked?
Elaine I finished your portrait.
Alaric I must see it.
Barton Because she was seeing a psychiatrist, wasn't she?
Alaric Yes.
Elaine I'll bring it to church tomorrow and show you.

Pause

Caroline enters

Caroline Did you bring that bottle of wine from the car?
Barton No.
Caroline Can you get it?
Barton In a minute.
Caroline Now. It should go in the fridge.

Barton follows Caroline into the house

Alaric I enjoyed the beach yesterday.
Elaine Yes, so did I. Do you think divorce harms the children?
Alaric It needn't.
Elaine Mmmm.
Alaric Yes. It was good to escape. Relax. I was feeling a bit tense.
Elaine Harold says I'm tense.
Alaric Been getting a bit irritable with Mother. Then I feel so guilty. I'm not a very good son, I'm afraid. I always feel a bit of a misfit when I come down here.

Elaine That's what Harold calls me — a misfit.
Alaric And then, of course, there's Barton being the dutiful nephew — just to make me feel worse.
Elaine Last night Harold and I had a bit of a row.
Alaric Oh dear.
Elaine Well, he gets a bit jealous.
Alaric Jealous?
Elaine Of my friends.
Alaric I see.
Elaine I suppose I make things difficult, really.
Alaric How come?
Elaine He says I'm abnormal.
Alaric Why?
Elaine I could do without the bed side of things altogether.
Alaric Maybe that's to do with him.
Elaine I don't know why I'm telling you all this.
Alaric I'm flattered you feel able to.

Margaret enters from the house

Margaret The food's nearly ready. Where's Tufty?
Elaine Down by the pond.
Margaret I might have known.
Elaine I'll go and get her.
Margaret Thank you.

Elaine exits

She's a funny thing, isn't she?
Alaric Mmmm. What's her husband like?
Margaret Bit hot-tempered.
Alaric Tufty seems nice.
Margaret Oh, yes she is.
Alaric Known her long?
Margaret She used to help look after my father. Meals on wheels. Home help. He thought the world of her.
Alaric Do you have friends in this area?
Margaret Who?
Alaric You and Tufty.

Act III 57

Margaret Most people we know are either from the choir or from work.
Alaric So no other gay friends?
Margaret I beg your pardon?
Alaric You don't have any lesbian friends.
Margaret No.
Alaric I just thought there might be some sort of group.
Margaret I've never been a person for groups.
Alaric No.

Pause

Margaret Actually, Michael Kingdom proposed to me.
Alaric Did he?
Margaret Yes.
Alaric His father used to drive the cattle lorry?
Margaret It's quite a thriving business now.
Alaric Really?
Margaret Of course, I refused.
Alaric Yes?
Margaret Too wide a gap.
Alaric Of course.
Margaret So there were others, Alaric.
Alaric I'm sure there were. (*Pause*) You always used to terrify me, you know? When we went out together.
Margaret Terrify you?
Alaric Yes, you made me feel that I had to be extremely sensible. No nonsense. You just weren't like other girls. You hated being flattered, I remember. You always seemed to see through me. It made me very edgy. Then when I saw you with Tufty, I understood.
Margaret Understood what, exactly?
Alaric Well, that you weren't really interested in men, sexually, I mean. That's why you didn't want to play all those courtship games. I think I sensed that even in those days.
Margaret How very observant of you.
Alaric I'm sorry, Margaret, have I offended you?
Margaret Not at all.
Alaric Oh, good.
Margaret I think you're rather jumping to conclusions.
Alaric Ah.

Margaret People are always so ready to do that, aren't they? They see two people living together and they make assumptions. When it's really none of their business.
Alaric I have offended you.
Margaret I just can't bear labels.
Alaric That's your right.
Margaret What is?
Alaric To define yourself in whatever way you choose.
Margaret I don't need to define myself, thank you.
Alaric That's what I meant.
Margaret I suppose you think we're rather grotesque.
Alaric No.
Margaret I know what goes on in people's heads. I mean, how dare people assume ... Who I live with is my business.
Alaric Of course it is.
Margaret Don't patronize me.
Alaric I'm sorry, I wasn't.
Margaret Oh, but I think you were. It's certainly not what you think. Some cosy quaint little ménage. The spinster schoolteacher living with her best friend and their dog.
Alaric No.
Margaret How dare you come down here and judge me and my life.
Alaric But I ——
Margaret You think I'm a failure, don't you? Just because I'm not married and I haven't got a job that impresses people. I chose to come back here and look after my father. No-one forced me. I like this town. I like being a primary school headmistress. Strange as it may seem to you. I'm happy in my work, in my life. I've no complaints, thank you. I certainly wouldn't want to be running around seeking prestige all the time. I don't need people's approval for the choices I've made in my life. I'm perfectly happy.

Tufty enters with Matt, Terry and Elaine

Tufty One of our little babies is dead.
Margaret What?
Tufty One of the ghost carp.
Margaret Oh, for goodness sake, stop harping on about your silly fish. The dinner's ready.

Act III   59

She exits

The others look after her. Black-out

                         THE GARDEN 2

Night

The slide show is in progress. Everyone is looking at the imaginary screen in the audience

Margaret That's Tufty on an elephant in Jaipur.

General response

Tufty You were so far off the ground. You could see why they used elephants for tiger hunting. It felt very safe.

Margaret After that we went to Varanassi. Benares as it used to be called by the British.

Tufty changes the slide to a landscape. There is general response to the new slide

Margaret This one's out of order, Tufty. It's Agra again. Taj Mahal.
Elaine I recognize that.

Tufty That's the view across the river from the back of the Taj.

Dulcie Beautiful, isn't it?

Margaret Tufty, it's slipped again. You can't see the people wading through the water at the bottom.
Tufty Help me move the book, then.
Margaret (*going to help her*) Sorry about this. Everyone OK? I hope we're not getting bitten by the midges. Tufty insisted on us sitting in the garden to look at the slides. I think she wanted you to get the genuine experience of India. Including getting eaten alive by insects.
Tufty It's cooler out here.
Barton I suppose you need to have a lot of jabs going somewhere like that.
Tufty Quite a few.

Margaret Hepatitis. Typhoid. Meningitis. Tetanus booster.
Tufty We decided not to have the cholera jab because it's only fifty per cent effective.
Margaret Malaria.
Tufty You had to take tablets all the time for that.
Dulcie The vicar before last, his daughter married a missionary and he got malaria out in Africa. Remember, Margaret?
Margaret I don't.
Dulcie It's a terrible disease.
Margaret Tufty?
Tufty What?
Margaret It still needs to go up.
Tufty I know.
Margaret This is Tufty's old projector that she's had for years and you can't adjust the legs properly.
Tufty Are you helping me or not?
Margaret There, can you see the people?
Barton Those little dots? I thought they were birds.
Margaret No, they're people.
Dulcie It keeps coming back, you see, malaria.
Margaret Next. Ah, now this is Varanassi. That's by the Ganges where they burn people when they die.
Dulcie Very public, isn't it?
Tufty There was a smell of hamburgers in the air. Bit unnerving.

General response

They just brush all the ashes and bits into the water afterwards.

Margaret They have a completely different attitude to death. It's not hidden away and sanitised. It's there, part of life.
Tufty And then people bathe in the water and wash their pots in it. It's a bit all-purpose, the Ganges.
Dulcie That must spread disease.

Tufty changes the slide

Margaret Hang on, Tufty, go back. I want to show them the little man who talked to us about reincarnation.

Act III

Tufty Sorry, memsahib. (*She changes the slide back*)
Margaret It's out of focus.
Tufty Blast.
Margaret I told you we should have borrowed the one from school. Anyone want another drink?
Dulcie Not for me, my dear.

Caroline gives Margaret her glass to be filled

Barton No thanks, not yet.
Terry Yes.
Dulcie He mustn't have any more.
Tufty I'll have one. (*She holds out her glass*)

Margaret looks at her and then takes it and goes and gets her a drink

Dulcie That wine we had with dinner's gone to my head.
Tufty (*fiddling with the projector*) Is that any good?
Margaret Not really. Shall I move the screen?
Tufty No.
Margaret That's better. More, more. No, it's gone out again. No, that's worse.
Barton You ought to get a video camera, Margaret.
Margaret Tufty, it's just getting more blurred.
Tufty I know. I'm trying to turn it the other way.
Margaret For goodness sake. That's better. That'll do.
Tufty Hang on.
Margaret That'll do. Leave it. It'll only go out again.
Tufty There we are.
Margaret Yes, there he is. He was a priest, I think. Reincarnation is fundamental to Hinduism. It's everyone's aim to be born at a higher level in their next life. And that depends how you lead this life. If you're not careful you can be born lower down the scale.
Tufty Finished?
Margaret Yes.
Matt (*putting his hand up*) Uh, Margaret?
Margaret Yes?
Matt Can I use your phone?
Caroline Matt! Don't be so rude.

Matt I want to phone Jason.
Barton Can't it wait?
Tufty Go ahead, Matt.
Matt No, it's all right.
Tufty You sure?
Matt Yeah.
Tufty (*changing the slide*) There's only a few left now. That's Varanassi again. (*She changes the slide*) Ganges. (*She changes the slide*) Ganges. (*She changes the slide*) Temple near Ganges.
Margaret Not so fast.

Tufty changes the slide

Dulcie Oh my, look at Margaret.
Barton That's what I call a candid shot.
Dulcie They're funny things those rickshaws, aren't they?
Margaret Yes.
Tufty Margaret didn't want me to show you this one. I must say I rather like it.
Barton It's like a motorbike with a cab on it.
Margaret That's what it is. Shall we carry on?
Caroline What's that hat you're wearing?
Tufty It was the only one we could find in the market.
Margaret Are there any more?
Tufty I think it suited her.
Barton Very fetching.
Margaret Can we carry on?
Tufty That was the last. (*She changes the slide*)

General response to the blank screen

Barton What were the roads like in India?
Caroline Why on earth do you want to know that?
Dulcie That was interesting. A real education.
Elaine Wonderful.
Caroline I'm surprised you could see anything with those sunglasses on. Did Alaric enjoy it?

Everyone looks at Alaric, who has fallen asleep. He suddenly starts

Act III   63

Alaric Pardon?
Barton You nodded off.
Alaric No I didn't.
Barton What was the last slide?
Alaric Ummm ...
Barton He doesn't know.
Alaric It was the elephant, wasn't it?

Laughter

Tufty That was no elephant, that was my wife.
Elaine The elephant was ages ago.
Tufty How many elephants can you get in a rickshaw?
Alaric I was watching.
Matt Can I phone Jason now?
Barton What's the hurry?
Matt I want to tell him about the studio.
Barton You've got to sort out that interview. You should phone up about that.
Caroline He can't do that at this time of night, can he?
Tufty Go on. You know where the phone is.

Matt exits

Elaine It's nice to see him smiling for a change.
Caroline You see, Alaric, you've brightened up all our lives.

Terry puts his arms around Alaric

Alaric Get off me, Terry, it's too hot.
Dulcie Leave him alone, Terry.
Alaric His mouth needs wiping.
Dulcie He's had too much to drink. Come here.

Terry goes to Dulcie to have his mouth wiped. Alaric helps himself to more punch

Alaric keeps on saying Terry should be working.

Alaric I didn't say that.
Dulcie You did.
Alaric I just think it might be good for him to be more independent.
Dulcie He couldn't do a job. Look at him.

Pause

Tufty Still so warm.
Dulcie Lovely for the holidaymakers.
Alaric It was beautiful on the beach yesterday.
Caroline I bet.
Alaric Look at at those stars. You don't see them like that in London.

Everyone looks up. A long silence

Elaine I'm not sure I believe in reincarnation.
Alaric No?
Elaine I prefer to believe that we become part of all that again when we die.
Alaric So you don't think the soul lives on?
Elaine I don't think the person who is me carries on.
Alaric Sounds like you're questioning the existence of the immortal soul. I don't know what your fundamentalist vicar would make of that.
Dulcie I know that your father is waiting for me.
Alaric What a morbid thought!
Dulcie It's true. Sometimes I know he's there. I can feel him.
Alaric He's had a long wait.
Dulcie You can laugh.
Tufty Oh dear.
Margaret What?
Tufty I hope I don't have to come back again.
Caroline Guess who Barton wants to come back as.
Barton Matt's running up Margaret's bill.
Caroline Go on, guess.
Elaine The vet on TV, what's his name?
Tufty I know the one you mean.
Caroline No, not him.
Dulcie The man that does the nature programme?
Caroline No.

Act III

Dulcie Attenborough.
Caroline No.
Margaret Saint Francis of Assisi.

Laughter

Caroline No.
Alaric Robert Redford.
Caroline Alaric's closest. He knows you, darling. Harrison Ford.

Everyone finds this hilarious

Tufty I can just see Barton doing all those stunts in *Raiders of the Lost Ark*.
Barton You're just jealous because you want to come back as Harrison Ford, too.
Tufty Do I? I've got this horrible feeling we wouldn't be able to choose. You might come back as a beggar in Calcutta.
Elaine No-one wants to be who they are, do they?

They all look at her

I mean, we're all looking for something else.
Alaric Our generation has got that particularly badly.
Elaine Yes?
Alaric Yes. I mean, we were actually very lucky with the time and place of our birth. We haven't had to suffer real hardship — not like those beggars. We've got healthcare, education, a good standard of living. Maybe our lives are too easy.
Tufty Speak for yourself.
Elaine It doesn't always feel easy.
Dulcie They didn't have penicillin when I was a child.
Alaric And we've never been through a war, either. We've lived through a period of comparative peace. And yet all the time we feel that something's missing.
Elaine Yes.
Dulcie My little brother died of scarlet fever.
Tufty What are you saying, Alaric? That you want a war to shake you out of yourself?

Alaric No. But I sometimes feel that nothing touches us, nothing can touch us.
Tufty Perhaps an earthquake, then.
Barton Or the collapse of the BBC.
Dulcie Wouldn't want to go back to those days. People don't know how lucky they are now. Washing machines and dishwashers. Want, want, want. More, more, more.
Alaric Mother, for God's sake! You talk too much.

Silence

Matt enters

Caroline Did you get through, darling?
Matt Yeah. Can I go over to see him?
Caroline Who?
Matt Jason.
Caroline At this time of night?
Barton It's ten miles.
Caroline It might be misty on the moors as well.
Alaric I'll take him.
Barton You mustn't.
Alaric I'd enjoy the drive.
Matt Thanks.
Barton You're not dragging Alaric all that way at this time of night.
Caroline You take him.
Barton No-one's taking him.
Alaric It's no problem. I'll be back in no time. Come on. Won't be long, Mother.
Dulcie Don't worry about me. I'm all right. I'll go and look at the fish pond. Anyway, Barton will give me a lift home.

Matt and Alaric start to leave. Caroline presents her face to be kissed. Matt kisses her

Matt (*to Barton*) Bye.

Barton doesn't respond. Terry goes and kisses Matt

Dulcie Come here, Terry.

Act III 67

Matt and Alaric exit

Elaine He's very excited, isn't he?
Tufty So much hope. He's just starting out.
Dulcie Yes.

They all look at her. Pause

Caroline Did you go to the beach with Alaric yesterday, Aunty?
Dulcie Oh no, my dear.
Caroline That's a shame. Didn't you want to go?
Dulcie I stayed at home and looked after Terry.
Caroline I thought he'd have taken you both.
Dulcie It was far too hot.
Caroline Did he go on his own, then?
Elaine I went with him.
Caroline Really? That was nice. I hope you didn't get burnt — what with your sensitive skin. (*To Barton*) You see, darling, I knew there'd be a good reason for her not coming round yesterday. Elaine comes to tea on Thursdays. It's our little routine.
Margaret Yes, I know.
Caroline I'm surprised you didn't go, Margaret. Oh, but you're busy getting ready for your little children, aren't you? Our lives must seem so uneventful to people like Alaric. We're bound up in our little world. Can hardly blame Elaine for running off to the beach with him.
Dulcie It was the hottest September day for twenty years, yesterday.
Caroline Barton really missed you, Elaine. He was quite grumpy when you didn't turn up, weren't you, darling?
Barton Not that I remember.
Caroline Oh, you were. You got quite short with me when I said that she didn't want to spend a nice hot day having tea with two old fogeys like us. He nearly bit my head off, Elaine.
Barton That's enough, darling.
Caroline I told him, familiarity breeds contempt. Who wants old friendships when there are new ones on the horizon?
Barton Caroline.
Caroline Oh, it looks as if I'm misbehaving. Naughty girl.
Dulcie The hottest place in England was Heathrow Airport. Course, it would be, with all that tarmac.

Caroline Doesn't Harold mind you spending all this time with Alaric?
Dulcie They'll be putting us on standpipes soon.
Caroline You're talking too much again, Aunty. Good job Alaric isn't here.
Barton Caroline.

Pause

Tufty Would you like to see the fish now, Mrs Barker?
Dulcie That would be lovely.

Tufty and Dulcie exit. Terry helps himself to some punch and then follows them

Caroline Charity obviously doesn't begin at home where Alaric's concerned.
Elaine Pardon?
Caroline Well, he doesn't seem to be putting himself out much for his mother and his brother.
Elaine He's being very kind to Matt.
Caroline Yes. I wonder what he's getting out of it. I suppose he's doing it to impress.
Elaine You ungrateful bitch.

Silence

Caroline bursts into tears and exits

Barton There go the waterworks again.

Margaret exits after Caroline

Elaine Maybe I should go and see if she's all right.
Barton Leave her. Margaret's gone.
Elaine I feel awful.
Barton She deserved it.
Elaine All the same ——
Barton Don't go. You've become a stranger this last week.
Elaine Don't you start.

Act III

Barton I've got to talk to you. Please.
Elaine What about?
Barton I want you to come away with me.
Elaine Where?
Barton Around the world.
Elaine You're mad.
Barton Yes, let's do something mad, before it's too late. There's nothing to keep us here. I've got some savings. I'm going to buy a motorbike and then we can just take off.
Elaine Barton!

He grabs her and kisses her. She struggles and pushes him away

What are you doing?
Barton I love you, Elaine.
Elaine Stop it. Stop it.

Pause

Barton It's because of him, isn't it?
Elaine Who?
Barton Alaric. You're so impressed by him, like everyone else. Did you hear him just now? He practically admitted that he's a phoney.
Elaine You're jealous.
Barton Yes, I'm jealous. I can hardly breathe when I think of you with him. I've been lying awake all night just thinking of you. I've been so stupid, I can't believe it. I've known you so long and I just didn't realize what you meant to me. I've wasted so much time. I can't think straight, I can't work. I was giving some inoculations this morning and I started to think of you and him, together, and my hand shook so much that I couldn't carry on. I had to tell the farmer that I was sick. And I am, in a way. Sick with love. I can't bear the thought of you being taken in by him. He's just bored. He'll pick you up and then drop you again when it suits him.
Elaine No-one's picking anyone up or dropping anyone. You seem to forget that I'm already married, Barton. Alaric and I enjoy each other's company. That's all. He's not the phoney. He's not the one who's deceiving his wife.
Barton At least I'm not deceiving myself as well.

He removes her sunglasses. She has a black eye

You trying to tell me you're happily married?
Elaine I'm going to find Caroline.

She puts the sunglasses back on again and exits

Barton is left on his own. He shakes his fist at the sky or hits himself. Eventually he pours himself a drink

Margaret enters

Margaret Has she come back?
Barton No.
Margaret I couldn't see her down there. I think she might have gone into the field.
Barton She'll be all right.
Margaret I hope so.
Barton Everyone's a bit jumpy tonight.
Margaret Yes.
Barton Do you remember those parties we used to have?
Margaret In the sixth form?
Barton Yes. There was always someone in the garden bawling their eyes out.
Margaret Or locked in the toilet.
Barton Mmmm.

Tufty enters

Tufty Mrs Barker's cross with Terry because he's drunk and Caroline's sitting all by herself in Webber's field. What's wrong with her?
Margaret Perhaps she wants to be on her own.
Tufty She seems upset. Someone should go and see if she's all right.

They both look at Barton

Barton Oh, OK.

Barton exits

Act III

Margaret Bit of inter-marital strife going on.
Tufty Not half.

Margaret starts to go

Sit with me.
Margaret What are the others doing?
Tufty Looking at the waterfall.

Margaret sits

I miss you. (*Pause*) Margaret.
Margaret What?
Tufty Talk to me.
Margaret What about?
Tufty I know you don't like talking about it.
Margaret About what?
Tufty Us.
Margaret Ughhh.
Tufty Maybe you're right. Maybe talking does no good. (*Pause*) But we do have some good times.
Margaret Of course we do.
Tufty So why aren't you happy?

Margaret does not respond

What do you want?
Margaret I don't know.

Pause. Tufty looks at her

(*Emphatically*) I don't know. (*Pause*) It wasn't meant to be like this. My life.

Pause

Dulcie and Terry enter

Dulcie Look at him. He's been sick in the pond.

Margaret Oh no.
Dulcie He doesn't know when to stop.
Tufty Come on, I'll take you indoors and clean you up.
Dulcie He's so sly. He must have been drinking when we weren't looking.

Tufty and Terry exit to the house

Margaret Put some music on while you're in there.
Dulcie I'm sorry, Margaret.
Margaret (*thinking she's referring to Terry*) You don't have to be.
Dulcie I know I talk too much.
Margaret (*realizing what she means*) Oh.
Dulcie I can't help it. It's because I get embarrassed. And now I've spoilt your dinner party.
Margaret No you haven't.

Dulcie cries. Music comes from inside the house: Placido Domingo singing "Our Love Is Here to Stay". Margaret attempts to comfort Dulcie, who continues crying

Barton enters and helps himself to another drink. After a moment Elaine wanders back. She and Barton avoid each other. After a moment Tufty and Terry return from the house

Tufty There's someone at the door.
Margaret Must be Alaric.

Tufty exits to the house

Dulcie I was beginning to wonder where he'd got to. Come on, Terry, we're going home now.
Margaret I must give you your trifle dish, Elaine.
Elaine Don't worry about that tonight.

The music is switched off abruptly. General response of regret

Tufty returns

Tufty Barton. Can you come, please?

Act III

Barton What is it?
Tufty It's someone for you.
Barton For me?

He exits with Tufty

Dulcie Isn't it Alaric?
Margaret Apparently not. (*She moves to look into the house*) It looks like a policeman.

Dulcie gasps

I'm sure it's nothing.
Dulcie Why's a policeman coming at this time of night?

Silence

Tufty returns

Tufty Can you get Caroline?
Margaret What's wrong?
Tufty Just get her.

Margaret exits

There's been an accident. They came off the road in the mist.
Dulcie I knew.
Tufty Alaric's fine, Mrs Barker. He's with the police. He's all right.
Dulcie Thank God.
Tufty It's Matt.
Elaine Oh no.
Tufty I'm afraid he's dead.

Margaret returns with Caroline. Pause

Caroline What's going on?

Barton enters from the house

Barton Caroline.

He returns into the house. Silence. Caroline looks at everyone and then follows him

The Lights fade

CURTAIN

ACT IV

*Early evening, two and a half years later. The Saturday before Christmas.
Behind the church looking at the graveyard*

A bench

Elaine and Alaric enter. Elaine is pushing a pram

Alaric She's sound asleep.
Elaine She always goes to sleep when you take her for a walk.
Alaric I still can't believe you're a grandmother.
Elaine You could have a grandchild. Miranda's older than Gwen.
Alaric True.
Elaine I don't feel like a grandmother.
Alaric It was a beautiful walk. Thank you.

They sit

What time does choir practice start?
Elaine Half past five. We're rehearsing the carol service.
Alaric Mmmm.
Elaine Are you going to come?
Alaric I told Mother I might.
Elaine That's wonderful. We need more basses.
Alaric All right. I'll come then.
Elaine What's your mother been doing this afternoon?
Alaric Christmas shopping with Tufty and Margaret. (*Pause*) So quiet up here.
Elaine Peaceful. (*Pause*) They've switched on the Christmas tree lights in the square.
Alaric I used to come up here sometimes after school.
Elaine On your own?
Alaric Yes. I was going through that moody adolescent phase. I used to sit up here and look down on it all. Watching the street lights come on.
Elaine Were you lonely?

Alaric I felt as if I didn't belong here. It all seemed so narrow and joyless. Drab. There's something so depressing about English towns.
Elaine Don't you think small towns are the same all over the world?
Alaric Maybe. I used to think I'd never escape.
Elaine So why do you want to come back and live here?
Alaric Hmmm?
Elaine If you find it so depressing.
Alaric I don't want to come and live here, actually in the town. We're looking at places near the sea.
Elaine Do you think your mother wants to move out of town?
Alaric She says she does. Why?
Elaine I just wondered.

Pause

Alaric Did you think of moving when you left Harold?
Elaine No. My job's here. And my children.
Alaric You ought to get away.
Elaine Why?
Alaric Pastures new.

Pause

Elaine I've got a Christmas present for you.
Alaric Oh, really?
Elaine (*taking a roll of paper from the pram*) Here.
Alaric This is a surprise. (*He unrolls the paper. It is the sketch of him on the moors*)
Elaine I always meant to send it to you and never got round to it.
Alaric (*looking at the sketch*) You put the deer in the background.
Elaine Yes.
Alaric Thank you. It's very flattering.

Elaine looks at it

Or perhaps I looked like that then. (*Pause*) It's like seeing someone from another age. I've changed so much since then.
Elaine Yes?
Alaric Oh yes.
Elaine I suppose I have, too. Now I'm on my own.

Act IV

Alaric You've still got the youngest two living with you?
Elaine Yes. And Gwen and little Eleanor live nearby.
Alaric Hmmm.
Elaine How's your daughter?
Alaric Miranda? She dropped out of University and is back living with her mother.
Elaine Oh no.
Alaric She came and visited me a few times in prison and I realized I didn't know how to talk to her anymore. She stopped coming in the end. I don't think she trusts me.
Elaine You mustn't give up.
Alaric No. That's one thing I decided in prison — to face up to my responsibilities: Mother ... Miranda ...
Elaine Terry?
Alaric Of course. (*Pause*) Afterwards, all I could think was, "Why wasn't it Terry? In the car with me?" Do you think that's awful?
Elaine No.
Alaric It's what I felt. (*Pause*) I wrote to Barton and Caroline, you know.
Elaine But you still haven't seen them since?
Alaric No. Mother said they've stopped coming to choir.
Elaine Yes.
Alaric What's the point of all this suffering, I wonder?

Terry enters

Hallo there. Where did you come from?
Terry Christmas.
Alaric Yes, it's Christmas.
Terry Christmas tree.
Alaric Down in the square. Can you see it?

Dulcie enters

Dulcie (*calling off*) They're round here. (*To Alaric and Elaine*) Wondered where you'd got to.
Elaine We're looking at the view.

Tufty and Margaret enter. Bruno is with them

Tufty That's our bench. Maggie and I used to sit there.

Dulcie Oh, this is Gwen's baby then. Isn't she lovely?
Tufty (*looking in the pram*) Hallo. What's your name, then?
Elaine Eleanor.
Tufty Hallo, little Eleanor. Aren't you good? Look, Maggie.
Margaret She's beautiful.
Dulcie Sit down, Terry. He's over-excited. He was driving me mad in the supermarket. Kept losing him. Here, let me wipe your nose. He's had this terrible cold for days. He caught it going down that garden centre — working in the cold. (*She wipes Terry's nose with a handkerchief*)
Alaric It's been quite mild.
Dulcie Alaric found out they wanted a bit of extra help so he persuaded them to take Terry on two days a week.
Alaric Did you get everything?
Dulcie Apart from the veg.
Tufty You'll be eating well over Christmas, I can tell you that.
Dulcie Ridiculous, isn't it, the amount of money we spend?
Margaret Yes. We'll never eat all we've bought.
Tufty We'll manage.
Dulcie People go mad. Spend, spend, spend.
Margaret What do you mean, "We'll manage"? You won't be here after Boxing Day.
Dulcie And the presents they buy. Little boy Webber next door to me is getting a computer. He's only six. And he's getting a bike from his grandparents.
Tufty Are you down for long, Alaric?
Alaric Just until we find somewhere we both like.
Tufty Oh, that's right. Mrs Barker was telling us.
Dulcie And she's just as bad, the mother. Her husband's got her a new cooker. The one they had was perfectly all right but it didn't go with the new fitted kitchen. So out it goes.
Alaric Mother, shhhh.
Dulcie Oh, sorry.
Tufty So your mother and Terry may be going to live with you.
Alaric They *are* going to. That's the whole idea.
Dulcie Do you think Mr Potter's arrived with the key yet?
Elaine I'll go and see.

Elaine exits

Dulcie They never used to lock the church.

Act IV

Margaret It's since the font was vandalized.
Dulcie What's the world coming to?
Tufty At least it's not quite as cold as it was.
Dulcie There's snow forecast. Perhaps we'll have a white Christmas.
Margaret I hope not.
Dulcie You'll have to think of us shivering in the snow while you're lying in the sun, Tufty.
Alaric (*to Margaret*) You going away?
Margaret Not me.
Dulcie Tufty's going to Spain for New Year.
Alaric Where in Spain?
Tufty A villa near Almeria.
Alaric Did some filming there once. It's beautiful. Going on your own?
Tufty No. With a friend. It's her villa.
Alaric It will be nice at this time of year.
Margaret I heard it can rain a lot.
Tufty Sit, Bruno.
Alaric Bruno's getting old.
Tufty Yes, we're a bit worried about him.
Margaret Let's hope he doesn't get worse while you're away.
Tufty Have you found a house you like yet?

During the following Terry moves to look in the pram

Alaric We looked at somewhere this morning but you weren't too keen, were you, Mum?
Dulcie It was too big. And the price they wanted for it!
Alaric Look, I told you not to worry about the price. Once I've sold the house in Blackheath it will more than cover it.
Dulcie It would be so much work to keep clean.
Alaric We'd be able to get someone in.
Dulcie Oh no. I want to do my own housework thank you very much. I'm not that old. Anyway, you said you wanted somewhere near the sea.
Alaric Well, the house we saw yesterday was right on the cliff.
Dulcie Oh, but it was so poky. You should have seen it, Margaret.
Alaric It wouldn't be too big to clean though, would it?
Dulcie Hmmm. Terry, come away from that baby! You'll give her your cold.

Elaine returns

Elaine There are a few more people there now. But Potter still hasn't turned up with the key.
Tufty We'll have to practice out here. How are you doing on your descant, Elaine?
Elaine "Once in Royal David's City" is still a bit shaky.
Margaret It's quite easy. (*She starts to sing the descant*)
Tufty (*over Margaret's singing; to Dulcie and Alaric*) I only have to sing the tune on that. They only ever give me the tune.

Elaine joins in singing

Margaret No.

They start again. Tufty joins in with the tune. Elaine goes wrong

(*To Tufty*) You're putting her off.
Tufty I was singing the tune. Sometimes it's easier if you sing the other part as well.
Margaret Not when you sing it off-key.

They start again. Dulcie joins in singing the tune

Elaine Darn.

Dulcie carries on singing

Margaret From the beginning again.

Dulcie continues singing

Alaric Mother.
Dulcie What?
Margaret I think it would be easier if we just sing the descant on its own, Mrs Barker.
Dulcie Sorry, my dear.

Margaret and Elaine sing the descant again. They manage to get through the first verse and start on the second verse. Dulcie and Tufty join in. They all laugh. Alaric claps

Act IV 81

Barton and Caroline enter. Caroline holds a bunch of flowers. Pause

Caroline That sounded very good.
Elaine We thought we'd practice out here seeing that we couldn't get into the church.
Barton Good idea.
Dulcie Lovely flowers.
Caroline Yes, aren't they? *(Pause)* This must be little Eleanor.
Elaine Yes.
Caroline Isn't she beautiful?
Barton Very bonny.

Pause

Tufty You coming to carol practice then, Barton?
Barton Yes, we thought we might.
Margaret We've missed your bass.
Tufty Potter hasn't arrived with the key yet.
Dulcie So we're locked out in the cold.
Barton Oh dear.
Dulcie And there's snow forecast.
Barton Yes, I heard.

Pause

Elaine New coat?
Caroline Yes.
Dulcie Very smart.
Tufty Christmas present?
Caroline Yes. From Barton.
Margaret Suits you.
Dulcie She's got lovely skin, hasn't she? Wish I had skin like that.
Caroline Thank you.

Pause

Tufty Perhaps someone ought to go and ask the vicar if we can borrow his key.
Elaine He doesn't like you disturbing him at teatime.

Tufty Well, it's not our fault Potter's so unreliable.

Pause

Barton How are you settling into your new house, Elaine?
Elaine It's all right. It's a bit cold.
Barton You ought to get on to the landlord. You should have central heating at the price you're paying.
Elaine The rent's about average for around here.
Dulcie I think it's daylight robbery.
Dulcie (*to Margaret*) Do you know how much she's paying?
Margaret Yes, it's scandalous.
Dulcie She ought to try and get somewhere cheaper.
Margaret That's what I said.
Dulcie The prices they charge. Lucky she's got a well-paid job.
Tufty You know there's a flat going down West Street overlooking the park, don't you?
Elaine No.
Barton That's a much better location.
Elaine I wouldn't want to move again.
Barton Bet it's cheaper.
Elaine Why does everyone want to tell me how to live my life now I'm on my own?
Barton Sorry.

Pause

Tufty Come on, Elaine. Let's go and face the vicar. I'll go if you go. He likes you.
Elaine All right. Keep an eye on the baby.
Dulcie We will.
Tufty No, Bruno. Stay.

Tufty and Elaine exit

Margaret It can't be easy.
Barton What?
Margaret Setting up home on your own after you've been married for all those years.
Caroline No.
Margaret Can I ask you a favour, Barton?

Act IV

Barton What's that?
Margaret Will you have a look at Bruno again sometime?
Barton I'll do it now.
Margaret Oh, thank you. Quick, while Tufty's not here.
Barton OK.
Margaret She hates me mentioning it, but I'm sure he's getting worse.
Barton Poor old boy. Let's have a look at you. (*He crouches down beside Bruno*)

Terry comes and watches

Caroline Have you been down long, Alaric?
Alaric About ten days.
Caroline Nice for you to have him here for Christmas, Aunty.
Dulcie Yes, it is.
Alaric It's good to be here.

Pause

Margaret That growth's getting bigger, isn't it?
Barton Yes. He's probably in pain.
Margaret He's off his food as well.
Barton You'd better think about bringing him in.
Margaret She's so fond of him. (*She cries*)

Pause

Dulcie Come away, Terry.
Alaric How old is he?
Margaret Eleven.
Dulcie That makes him seventy-seven, doesn't it?
Barton It doesn't really work like that.
Dulcie That's what they always say. Multiply the age by seven.
Barton He's old for a dog.

Dulcie shivers

Margaret Would you like to go and wait in the car, Mrs Barker? You'll be warmer there.
Alaric That's a good idea, Mother.

Dulcie What about the baby?
Alaric Oh, ummm ...
Dulcie At least she's wrapped up warm.
Caroline We'll watch her.
Alaric Thanks.
Dulcie Come on then, Terry.
Margaret And you, Bruno.

Margaret, Alaric, Dulcie and Terry exit

Caroline looks in the pram. Barton sits in silence

Caroline Elaine warned me he was coming down.
Barton Yes.
Caroline You knew?
Barton Aunty phoned me at work.
Caroline You didn't tell me. (*Pause*) He can't have been back for ages.
Barton No.
Caroline Not since the court case. Two years.

Barton picks up the sketch and looks at it

What's that?
Barton Nothing. (*He rolls it up and puts it to one side*) Did you get a turkey?
Caroline No, I didn't bother.
Barton Don't you want one?
Caroline I suppose we should have one.
Barton Farmer over at Verraby gave me one today.
Caroline That was kind. (*Pause*) Elaine says he's going to buy a house down here.
Barton Alaric?
Caroline Yes. Didn't Aunty tell you? She and Terry are going to live with him.
Barton Here in town?
Caroline No. Somewhere by the sea.

Pause

Barton I could get a tree as well.

Act IV

Caroline What?
Barton A Christmas tree. I could get one tomorrow.
Caroline Do we have to have a tree?
Barton Not if you don't want to.
Caroline They make so much mess. (*Pause*) I hate Christmas.
Barton Don't——
Caroline I don't know why we came.
Barton You miss the choir.
Caroline Do you think he'll be coming carol singing with us?
Barton Who, Alaric? I shouldn't think so. (*Pause*) Maybe we should have him over.
Caroline Why?
Barton I don't know. Aunty would be pleased.
Caroline No. (*Pause*) Are you going to take the flowers down to the grave or shall I?
Barton I will. Won't be long.

Barton picks up the flowers and exits

Caroline sits looking at the baby. She sings, under her breath, the first two lines of "Eleanor Rigby" by The Beatles. Then she stops, lost in thought

Elaine enters

Elaine Is she all right?
Caroline Yes.
Elaine Where is everyone?
Caroline They've taken Aunty to the car to keep warm. Did you get the key?
Elaine The vicar wasn't there. Tufty's gone to look for Mr Potter.
Caroline Bit of a disaster. (*Pause*) He doesn't look any different, does he?
Elaine Alaric?
Caroline Yes.
Elaine No, he doesn't.
Caroline Be nice to have a house by the sea.
Elaine Wonder if he'll do it.
Caroline What?
Elaine Move back here.
Caroline I was surprised.

Elaine We'll see.
Caroline You shouldn't let Barton annoy you like that, you know.
Elaine I know.
Caroline He means well.
Elaine I know. Where is he anyway?
Caroline He's taken the flowers to the grave. (*Pause*) Christmas is the worst time.
Elaine I'm sure.
Caroline I was thinking of the year we bought him his first guitar. And a Beatles songbook. The three of us sat by the fire singing all afternoon.
Elaine He had a lovely voice.

Pause. Elaine takes her hand

Caroline At least I don't want to lie down and die anymore. You've got to carry on living, haven't you? Might have to come back and do it again otherwise.

Margaret and Alaric return

Alaric I'm sorry. I forgot something. (*He looks for the sketch*)
Caroline There was nothing on the bench.
Alaric Perhaps it's fallen down behind.
Caroline Oh, there was this. (*She holds up the rolled-up sketch*)
Alaric That's it.
Caroline What is it?
Elaine It's a sketch I did.
Caroline Can I see? (*She unrolls it*)

Margaret joins her

Margaret Oh, very good.
Caroline It's a good likeness. (*She rolls it up and hands it to Alaric*)
Margaret Still no key?
Elaine No. Tufty's gone off to find Potter.
Margaret She'll be lucky.
Caroline Excuse me.

Caroline exits

Act IV

Elaine Oh dear.
Alaric What?
Elaine I wish she hadn't seen it.
Alaric I shouldn't have left it there. I'm sorry.
Elaine It's not your fault.
Alaric I think I should go home.
Margaret You should stay.
Alaric I wouldn't have come if I'd known they were going to be here.
Margaret You can't go through life feeling guilty.
Alaric No?
Margaret It was an accident.
Alaric That's not what the judge thought.
Margaret The judge was biased against you.
Alaric I had been drinking.
Margaret It's always tragic when someone so young dies. But it happens.
Alaric I feel as if I've opened the wound.
Margaret The rest of us just get older and greyer and sadder. Perhaps that's our tragedy.
Elaine They thought of moving.
Margaret Who?
Elaine Barton and Caroline.
Alaric Really?
Elaine But they didn't.
Margaret No.
Elaine Wherever you go, you take yourself with you.

Tufty enters

Tufty Well, I can't find the vicar or Potter. So we need to have a little conflab with the others out the front. They're getting restless. They want to know how much longer we're going to wait.
Margaret All right.

Elaine goes to get the baby

Alaric Leave her with me while you do that.
Margaret Aren't you coming?
Alaric I'll wait to see what you decide.

Tufty, Margaret and Elaine exit

Alaric sits. He looks at the sketch

Barton enters and sits beside Alaric. Pause

Barton It's getting dark.
Alaric Yes.
Barton I'm sure I saw a snowflake just now.
Alaric I did too. (*Pause*) They're having a little meeting because they still can't get in.
Barton Sign of the times, isn't it?
Alaric What?
Barton A locked church.

Alaric smiles

Not that I've wanted to go into churches much lately.
Alaric No?
Barton No.
Alaric Funny, that.
Barton Why?
Alaric I went and stayed in a monastery this summer. On a retreat.

They laugh

Barton So you're returning to your roots?
Alaric Maybe.
Barton Big change for you, coming back here.
Alaric Yes.
Barton Won't you find it a bit quiet?
Alaric I don't know. I thought that was what I wanted.
Barton A bit of quiet?
Alaric Yes.
Barton A bit of peace.
Alaric Yes.

Pause

Barton Well, I can't say I've forgiven you.

Act IV

Alaric No.
Barton But I don't feel the same rancour. Not anymore. Towards you. (*Pause*) As long as I blamed you, I didn't have to face up to my own remorse. Awful thing, isn't it? Remorse.
Alaric Yes.
Barton Yes.
Alaric And how's Caroline?

Pause

Barton We'll look after your Mum and Terry, you know. I know we haven't seen much of them the last couple of years but they're family.
Alaric Oh, but I'm ——
Barton So if you're worried about them down here on their own, you don't have to be.
Alaric Right.
Barton We won't abandon them. (*Pause*) That was definitely a snowflake.
Alaric It was.

It begins to snow lightly

Dulcie enters with Terry. She is embarrassed to see Barton and Alaric together

Dulcie Oh, I was looking for the others.
Alaric They're round the front.
Dulcie It's snowing.
Alaric We know.
Dulcie There's no point hanging around anymore.
Barton I'll go and see what they've decided.

Barton exits

Dulcie I'm worried about Terry's chest. Look at his hands, he's blue.
Alaric (*to Terry*) Oh yes, you're freezing, aren't you? Let me warm you up.
Dulcie He can't carry on with this job if he's going to get ill.

Alaric rubs Terry's hands together

Alaric Brrrrr.
Dulcie Don't be too rough with him.
Alaric Stamp your feet.
Dulcie You and Barton have a chat?
Alaric Yes. Come on, get that circulation going. Now let's go for a little run.

Terry and Alaric run around the bench. Alaric sings to Terry to the tune of "Singing in the Rain"

Dulcie Careful ...
Alaric (*singing*) We're running in the snow,
　　　　　　　Just running in the snow ...
Dulcie Was that all right?
Alaric What?
Dulcie Your chat with Barton.
Alaric (*stopping*) Yes. I think so. (*He sits on the bench and hugs Terry*)
Dulcie I'm glad you talked. Especially if you're going to come and live down here. (*She goes and checks the pram*) She's still warm as toast in there. (*Seeing the baby is startled*) Oh, I'm sorry. Did I frighten you? (*She tries to console the baby*)
Alaric I had a letter from an old friend at the BBC. He wants me to do some work on a new series of documentaries.
Dulcie Oh yes?
Alaric It would mean being in London a lot.
Dulcie I see.
Alaric I wasn't going to reply.
Dulcie You must.
Alaric It might mean postponing any move.
Dulcie Oh dear. Well, your work's got to come first.
Alaric Yes.
Dulcie You can always come and visit.
Alaric Mmmm.
Dulcie Need my umbrella. (*She puts up an umbrella*) Here, Terry, put your hat on.

Alaric puts Terry's hat on for him

Alaric Do you mind?

Act IV

Dulcie You must do what's best for you.
Alaric But what about you?
Dulcie I'm all right. You mustn't worry about me.
Alaric I do.
Dulcie Tell you the truth, Al, I think we'd be happier staying here in the town.
Alaric I see.
Dulcie We're all right, aren't we, Terry?
Terry Snow.
Dulcie Yes. Isn't it pretty?
Alaric Can I have his hanky?

Dulcie hands him the handkerchief

Alaric (*holding it to Terry's nose*) Blow. (*He wipes Terry's nose*)

Elaine enters and goes to the pram

Elaine Still no sign of Potter.
Dulcie Don't worry. She's all right.

Tufty, Margaret and Barton return

Margaret Do you want a lift home, Mrs Barker?
Barton (*calling*) Caroline!
Tufty That's snow, little Eleanor.
Barton (*calling*) Caroline.
Caroline (*off*) Coming.

Elaine picks up the baby

Tufty (*to the baby*) You haven't seen that before, have you?
Elaine She doesn't know what to make of it.

They all stand in the snow waiting for Caroline

   Caroline enters

Caroline The hills are completely white already.

Margaret So they are.

They stand watching

 It's like a Victorian Christmas card.
Elaine (*singing quietly*) Snow had fallen,
      Snow on snow,

Dulcie joins in

     Snow on snow.

Tufty joins in

     In the bleak midwinter
     Long ago.

They laugh. An organ starts to play. They look at each other

Barton Someone's got into the church.
Tufty Just as we were beginning to give up.

Pause

Margaret Let's go and sing then.
Elaine Are you joining us, Alaric?
Alaric No. I thought I'd take a little walk.
Dulcie You wrap up.
Alaric I'll come back for you, Mother.
Dulcie That'll be nice.

Everyone but Alaric heads off to the church. They start singing

     In the bleak midwinter,
     Frosty winds made moan.
     Earth stood hard as iron,
     Water like a stone.
     Snow had fallen,
     Snow on snow,

Act IV

> Snow on snow,
> In the bleak midwinter,
> Long, long ago.

Alaric stands listening

   Matt enters and joins him

The snow continues to fall on the stage, thickly covering it in white. The Lights fade

CURTAIN

FURNITURE AND PROPERTY LIST

ACT I

On stage: Table
Chairs
Telephone
Coat
Sherry glasses

Off stage: Towel (**Dulcie**)
Terry's clothing (**Dulcie**)
Biscuit tin with biscuits (**Dulcie**)
Glass of soda pop (**Dulcie**)
Sandwich (**Dulcie**)
Carrier bag containing a bottle of sherry (**Tufty**)
Glass of water (**Barton**)
Bag containing slides (**Margaret**)
5 teacups (**Caroline**)
Teapot (**Dulcie**)
Cloth (**Dulcie**)

Personal: **Caroline:** Handbag. *In it:* money, compact

ACT II

On stage: Blanket
Apples
Sweater

Off stage: Frisbee (**Matt**)
Towels (**Matt**)
Bathing costume (**Matt**)
Folding chair (**Alaric**)
Blanket (**Alaric**)

Personal: **Tufty:** pack of cigarettes and lighter
Margaret: rucksack. *In it:* bathing costume, towels, can of beer
Dulcie: bag containing food, orange juice, towels, etc.

Elaine: sketching materials
Tufty: car keys

ACT III

On stage: Garden table and chairs
Punchbowl and glasses
Slide projector (practical)
Slide cassette with slides
Step ladder

Off stage: Book (**Margaret**)

Personal: **Elaine:** ostentatious sunglasses, handbag containing compact and lipstick
Dulcie: handkerchief

ACT IV

On stage: Bench

Off stage: Pram (**Elaine**)
Rolled up sketch (**Elaine**)

Personal: **Dulcie:** handkerchief, umbrella
Caroline: bunch of flowers
Terry: hat

LIGHTING PLOT

Practical fittings required: nil
Interior and exterior settings

ACT I

To open: General interior lighting

No cues

ACT II

To open: General exterior lighting

Cue 1	They all sit or stand in silence *The lights dim to indicate the passage of time*	(Page 39)
Cue 2	When ready *Bring up lights*	(Page 39)
Cue 3	**Elaine:** "At least someone's happy." *The lights fade*	(Page 48)

ACT III

To open: General effect of early evening

Cue 4	**Margaret** exits; the others look after her *Black-out*	(Page 59)
Cue 5	When ready *Bring up lights to evening effect*	(Page 59)
Cue 6	**Caroline** follows **Barton** into the house *The lights fade*	(Page 74)

ACT IV

To open: General effect of early winter evening

Cue 7   **Matt** enters and joins **Alaric**   (Page 93)
         The lights fade

EFFECTS PLOT

ACT I

Cue 1	**Terry:** "Later." *Doorbell*	(Page 5)
Cue 2	**Terry** goes to the biscuit tin and takes a biscuit *Telephone rings*	(Page 5)
Cue 3	**Caroline:** "And she told me she was embarrassed." *Doorbell*	(Page 9)
Cue 4	**Barton:** "A freelance producer and director." *Doorbell*	(Page 20)
Cue 5	**Caroline** sobs *Sound of a brass band*	(Page 25)
Cue 6	**Alaric:** "I couldn't get through." *The brass band music gets louder*	(Page 25)

ACT II

No cues

ACT III

Cue 7	**Dulcie** cries *Music: "Our Love Is Here to Stay" comes from inside the house*	(Page 72)
Cue 8	**Elaine:** "Don't worry about that tonight." *Cut music*	(Page 72)

ACT IV

Cue 9　**Alaric:** "It was."　(Page 89)
　　　　Snow effect, starting lightly and gradually becoming heavier throughout the rest of the scene

Cue 10　**Elaine, Dulcie** and **Tufty** laugh　(Page 92)
　　　　Organ music

A licence issued by Samuel French Ltd to perform this play does not include permission to use the Incidental music specified in this copy. Where the place of performance is already licensed by the Performing Right Society a return of the music used must be made to them. If the place of performance is not licensed than application should be made to the PERFORMING RIGHT SOCIETY, 29 Berners Street, London W1.

A separate and addition licence from PHONOGRAPHIC PERFORMANCES LTD, Ganton House, Ganton Street, London W1, is needed whenever commercial recordings are used.

MADE AND PRINTED IN GREAT BRITAIN BY
LATIMER TREND & COMPANY LTD PLYMOUTH
MADE IN ENGLAND